Comparative
Psychology

Comparative Psychology

PHYLETIC DIFFERENCES IN BEHAVIOR

by David Lester

Alfred
PUBLISHING CO., INC

Library of Congress Catalog Card Number: 72-95492

ISBN: 0-88284-004-5

Printed in the United States of America

Alfred Publishing Co., Inc.
75 Channel Drive, Port Washington, New York 11050

To Gene

Contents

Acknowledgments

I WOULD LIKE to thank Dr. Julian Jaynes and Dr. Douglas Candland for comments on an early draft of this book. I would like especially to thank Dr. Gene Lester for assisting me in editing and writing the book.

In addition I would like to thank the following authors and publishers for allowing me to reproduce figures and tables from their works:

Table 3.1   From H. H. Ross, *Understanding evolution.* Englewood Cliffs: Prentice-Hall, 1966. By permission of the publisher, Prentice-Hall.

Figures 4.1, 4.2, and 4.3   From C. A. Villee, W. F. Walker, and F. E. Smith. *General zoology.* Philadelphia: Saunders, 1963. By permission of the publisher, W. B. Saunders, and Dr. C. Villee.

Figure 6.1   From G. L. Walls. The vertebrate eye and its adaptive radiation. *Cranbrook Institute of Science Bulletin,* 1942, volume 19. By permission of the publisher, Weidenfeld and Nicolson.

Figure 6.2   From R. L. Gregory. *Eye and brain.* New York: McGraw-Hill, 1966. By permission of the publisher, McGraw-Hill.

Figure 6.3   From P. Marler and W. J. Hamilton. *Mechanisms of animal behavior*. New York: Wiley, 1966. By permission of the publisher, John Wiley.

Figure 7.1   From R. D. Walk and E. J. Gibson. A comparative and analytical study of visual depth perception. *Psychological Monographs,* 1961, 75, #15. By permission of the publisher, The American Psychological Association.

Figure on page 82.   From G. A. Mazokhin-Porshnyakov. *Insect vision*. New York: Plenum, 1969. By permission of the publisher, Plenum Press.

Figure 7.3   From B. J. Fellows. *The discrimination process and development*. New York: Pergamon, 1968. By permission of the publisher, Pergamon Press, and Mr. B. J. Fellows.

Table 9.1   From J. P. Scott. Animal sexuality. In A. Ellis and A. Abarbanel (eds.) *Encyclopedia of sexual behavior*. New York: Hawthorn, 1961. By permission of the publisher, Hawthorn Books.

Table 10.1   From J. P. Scott. The social psychology of infrahuman animals. In G. Lindzey and E. Aronson (eds.) *The handbook of social psychology,* volume I. Reading, Mass.: Addison-Wesley, 1969. By permission of the publisher, Addison-Wesley.

Figure 13.1   From W. Hodos. Evolutionary interpretation of neural and behavioral studies of living vertebrates. In F. O. Schmitt (ed.) *The neurosciences: second study program*. New York: Rockefeller University Press, 1970. By permission of the publisher, The Rockefeller University Press, and Dr. W. Hodos.

Figure on page 168.   From N. Tinbergen. *The study of instinct*. London: Oxford University Press, 1951. By permission of the publisher, The Oxford University Press.

1
Introduction

Chapter 1

Introduction

Several recent books on animal behavior bear titles referring to "comparative psychology." Though these books contain vast quantities of information on the behavior of different animals, they rarely take a genuinely *comparative* approach. Data about the behavior of different species are given, but not compared. Denny and Ratner, in their book on comparative psychology (1970), presented some 800 pages of original discussion, abstracts of articles on animal behavior, and reprints of articles. Occasionally they pointed to trends in the behavior of difference between species belonging to different phyla. But most of the book is taken up with material which might be summarized as "the monkey does this and the rat does that, while on the other hand the ant does this." At the end, one is left with many pieces of information but little "comparative" organization. In fact, though Denny and Ratner reprinted some 50 articles, 43 were concerned with only one species, while seven were concerned with several members of one genus or family. No study was reprinted comparing several diverse species from different orders, classes, or phyla. (There is no intention here to single out Denny's and Ratner's book for special criticism. It is a well-respected volume which accurately represents the state of comparative psychology, which is my reason for remarking on it.)

This book will not attempt to make an exhaustive presentation of the results of research in animal behavior. Rather, its aim is to *illustrate* behavioral trends that can be noted when different species are compared.

To be sure, a detailed exploration of the behavior of each species is necessary. But some psychologists are impatient with this thorough, systematic approach and would like to anticipate the conclusions of a truly comparative psychology. This book is devoted to such anticipation.

The book may be viewed in two ways. First, it may be used as an *introduction* to the study of comparative psychology, to orient the student initially before he moves on to the more detailed investigation of particular topics, either in the library or in the laboratory. Second, it may be used as a *supplementary text*, to accompany one of the several fine books available on animal behavior. Two outstanding books on animal behavior are those by Hinde (1970) and Marler and Hamilton (1966). Both describe in detail the behavior of different animal species and are written from a reasonably unbiased point of view.

Why Study Animal Behavior?

Psychologists are often asked why they study the behavior of animals. Some writers define psychology as the study of behavior, a definition that would naturally include the study of animal, as well as human, behavior. Perhaps it is only because psychology includes the study of man that people sometimes take an anthropocentric point of view and argue that the study of animal behavior is important only if it aids us in our understanding of man.

The fact that the study of animal behavior is of intrinsic

interest does not mean that such study cannot facilitate our understanding of man's behavior. In Chapter 14 I illustrate some general ways in which we might learn about human beings from the study of animals. In addition to the general parallels that are discussed in that chapter, the study of animals aids the study of man in several concrete ways:

1. Animals, especially those reared for laboratory use, tend to be genetically more similar to each other than do individual members of the human species. This greater homogeneity reduces the individual variability between members of the species and renders the study of a particular behavior more feasible. For example, we tend to study the physiological mechanisms that control eating behavior in rats or dogs, while in man we study individual differences in eating behavior.

2. Ethical considerations prevent us exploring the effect of physiological manipulations (such as brain lesions) and severe behavioral manipulations (such as sensory deprivation) in man. The use of animals allows such studies to be carried out. Furthermore, because we can rear the animal in the laboratory and completely control its experience, we can more easily tease out the particular variables responsible for the control of a behavior in an animal than we can in man.

3. Psychological understanding of behavior has far to go. Starting with an organism as complex as man may prevent us from ever gaining a glimmer of understanding about behavior. Just as the child crawls before he walks (usually) or learns to play checkers before he learns to play chess, so some psychologists often begin with a supposedly simpler animal species (the rat, for example) before tackling the same behavior in man. As we will discover in this book, because animals resemble man in many ways, we can learn about one from the study of the other.

The Organization of This Book

Part I introduces the reader to some basic concepts in taxonomy and evolution. These concepts are intimately related to some issues in comparative psychology. The discussion is not intended to be exhaustive; the reader with a background in biology may find it possible to pass it by.

The material in Part II stresses the fact that behavior is crucially dependent on the structure and physiology of the animal. It is possible to carry out an analysis of the behavior of one species or of several at a purely behavioral level, but some researchers prefer to relate behavioral qualities to physiological qualities. Part II illustrates some comparative trends in anatomy and physiology that are of interest.

The meat of the book lies in Parts III and IV, in which I discuss some of the comparative trends that have been identified, along with some of the criticisms and issues raised in connection with comparative psychology.

To some extent, my choice of material is a bit whimsical. I have included material on comparative psychology rarely found in other books; it simply tickled my fancy. I hope such digressions will be justified by the aroused interest of the reader.

What Is the Phyletic Scale?

In addition to having the subtitle "phyletic differences in behavior," this book carries the word *phyletic* on nearly every page, often as part of the phrase "phyletic scale." What is this scale?

The phyletic scale is a fiction, but nevertheless a fiction that has a degree of reality. In the past the many species of animals have been ordered in a way which seems to make sense and which different investigators agree on. When one tries to order the phyla in terms of complexity or development, the chordates appear on top and the protozoa at the bottom. When one tries to order the vertebrates, the sequence runs from the mammals, through the birds, reptiles, and amphibia, down to the fish. Within the mammalian class, the primates are considered to be at the top, followed by the carnivores and the rodents.

In the past, this ordering was called the "phylogenetic scale," a term which has several implications. The first is that animals close together on the scale are similar from an evolutionary point of view; that is, they have a common ancestor which lived relatively recently on the biological time scale. Second, it was sometimes implied that species higher on the phylogenetic scale had evolved from species lower on the scale. For example, man is higher in the phylogenetic scale than the monkeys and the apes, so it has been thought by some that perhaps man descended or evolved from an ape. (Although man and the apes we know today are probably descended from some common ancestor or set of ancestors, no man living today is descended from an ancestor belonging to any of the species of apes which exist today.)

In recent years the concept of a phylogenetic scale has come under attack from psychologists who argue that the implications contained in the concept are erroneous. (Some of these criticisms are discussed in Chapter 13.) For this reason it has become dangerous to use the term "phylogenetic scale," for to do so leaves one open to attack from these psychologists. We need a new term, one that is neutral and has no misleading connotations. In this book I have used the term "phyletic scale" to mean simply *a scale ordered in terms of the differential characteristics of different species.**

The concept of the phyletic scale simplifies describing the kinds of animals about which a particular conclusion is made. One can talk of "lower" and "higher" animals, meaning "animals toward the protozoa end of the phyletic scale, compared to those at the primate end of the phyletic scale," and

---

* For example, their ease of learning a habit reversal task (see Chap. 8).

thereby economize on space. I have tried to consistently use the terms "lower" and "higher" in this context. Other researchers often talk of *simple* and *complex* animals or of *primitive* and *nonprimitive* animals.

What is the basis for the ordering of the phyletic scale? It would seem that there is none. Yet it is an ordering that seems to make sense. The major reason for the use of the concept in this book is convenience.

It will perhaps be a measure of the success of comparative psychology during the next few decades if we discover a rational basis on which to order the different species of animals, a basis that will enable us to discard the concept of the "phyletic scale," or alternatively, to provide an empirical foundation for the ordering the scale uses.

References

Denny, M. R.; and Ratner, S. C. 1970. *Comparative psychology.* Homewood, Ill.: Dorsey Press.

Hinde, R. A. 1970. *Animal behavior.* New York: McGraw-Hill.

Marler, P.; and Hamilton, W. 1966. *Mechanisms of animal behavior.* New York: Wiley.

Chapter 2

The Zoological Classification of Animals*

WHEN WE LOOK at the behavior of different animals we are going to run into the problem of determining how similar (or how different) the animals are. For example, if we find that two strains of rats differ in performing some learning task, we will view the implications and importance of this difference very differently than if we were to find the same difference in performance between a rat and a flatworm, two animals that belong to different phyla.

Zoologists who deal with the problem of describing and classifying animals are known as taxonomists. The schema they have produced constitutes the only extensive, systematic attempt at classification presently available. Consequently, comparative psychologists have used the schema to help them identify the degree of similarity between the different animals they have studied.

In this chapter I will describe the principle behind zoological taxonomy and describe the schema used in classification.

---

* In this chapter I draw extensively from Mayr (1969) and to a lesser extent from Villee et al. (1963) and Waters et al. (1960).

Categories of Animals

There are two kingdoms of living organisms: the plant kingdom, which at present is known to constitute about a half million different species, and the animal kingdom, which includes about 1 million different species. Estimates of the number of undescribed species range from 3 million to 10 million. There are also an estimated 500 million species that are now extinct. The task of classifying all this is immense.

Taxonomy consists of at least two distinct tasks. The first is the identification of species. A particular species of animal may look quite different at various ages. The two sexes may differ in appearance and behavior. The appearance of individuals may also be affected by such factors as climate. The taxonomist has to identify which particular organisms and forms of these organisms are different forms of the same species and which are different species. Having identified a species, the taxonomist must then classify it. This involves trying to ascertain the relationship between the newly identified species and species which were previously known, by deciding how similar the new species is to other species and in what ways it is different.

Each animal is assigned two names by the taxonomist. The first name describes the genus to which it belongs, while the second identifies the species. The genus is always a noun —for example, *Canis* (dog) and *Perca* (perch)—and is always capitalized. A particular genus name can be used only once in the entire animal kingdom; duplication between the animal kingdom and the plant kingdom is discouraged. The species name is not capitalized and may be an adjective or a noun. It serves to identify a particular group within a genus and thus may be used in different genera. For example, *Cylichna alba* is a white snail and *Fredericia alba* is a white worm.

How does a taxonomist define a species? The members of a species are defined as a group of animals which under natural circumstances will interbreed with each other and not interbreed with other groups. The barriers between species may involve discrepancies in genetic material, size differences, behavioral peculiarities, or simply geographical isolation. Under unnatural circumstances, members of two different species can sometimes mate; the resulting hybrids are usually sterile or of lowered viability. Occasionally, however, a breakdown of isolation between species creates new populations which may or may not develop in time into new species.

The species is the most basic taxonomic category. Definition of the categories higher in the taxonomic hierarchy is essentially pragmatic. For example, a genus may be defined as a taxonomic category containing one or more species which is separated from other genera by a "decided gap." This definition is somewhat imprecise, in that what constitutes a "decided gap" may be a matter of opinion. But insofar as taxonomists agree on the identification and classification of genera, the definition is useful.

In the same way the next higher category—the family—is defined, and so on. The basic taxonomic schema consists of seven categories arranged hierarchically:

Kingdom
  Phylum
    Class
      Order
        Family
          Genus
            Species

Only the species has an objective and operational definition. Opinion plays a part in decisions made about what fits in where in the higher taxonomic categories.

Every species is thus assigned to particular groups of these seven categories. The following examples will illustrate this, as well as show the extent of the difference between animals that differ in their species, genus, family, and so forth:

11

Basic Taxonomic Schema

	COYOTE	WOLF	AFRICAN SAND FOX	TIGER
kingdom	Animalia	Animalia	Animalia	Animalia
phylum	Chordata	Chordata	Chordata	Chordata
class	Mammalia	Mammalia	Mammalia	Mammalia
order	Carnivora	Carnivora	Carnivora	Carnivora
family	Canidae	Canidae	Canidae	Felidae
genus	*Canis*	*Canis*	*Vulpes*	*Panthera*
species	*latrans*	*lupus*	*pallida*	*tigris*

	FINBACK WHALE	BULLFROG	HONEY BEE
kingdom	Animalia	Animalia	Animalia
phylum	Chordata	Chordata	Arthropoda
class	Mammalia	Amphibia	Insecta
order	Cetacea	Anura	Hymenoptera
family	Balaenopteridae	Ranidae	Apidae
genus	*Balaenoptera*	*Rana*	*Apis*
species	*physalus*	*catesbeiana*	*mellifera*

As more and more species have been identified, the need for additional categories has arisen, so a number of sub-categories have been adopted for general usage. The generally accepted categories are:

kingdom
  phylum
    subphylum
      superclass
        class
          subclass
            cohort
              superorder
                order

suborder
  superfamily
    family
      subfamily
        tribe
          genus
            subgenus
              species
                subspecies

I state above that there are about a million living species of animals presently identified and classified. These species are distributed among 24 phyla. The distribution of these species among the phyla is:

PHYLUM		NUMBER OF SPECIES
Protozoa	(protozoans)	28,350
Mesozoa		50
Porifera	(sponges)	4,800
Coelenterata	(polyps and medusae)	5,300
Ctenophora	(comb jellies)	80
Platylhelminthes	(flatworms)	12,700
Entoprocta		75
Nemertinea	(ribbon worms)	800
Aschelminthes		12,500
Priapulida		8
Mollusca	(molluscs)	107,250
Sipunculida		250
Echiurida		150
Annelida	(segmented worms)	8,500
Onychophora		70
Tardigrada		350
Pentastomida		65
Arthropoda	(arthropods)	838,000
Lophorata		3,750
Hemichordata		80
Echinodermata		6,000
Pogonophora		100
Chaetognatha	(arrow worms)	50
Chordata	(vertebrates, sea squirts, and lancelets)	43,000
		1,072,278

The majority of the animals studied by comparative psychologists come from five of these phyla (Platyhelminthes, Mollusca, Annelida, Arthropoda, and Chordata). The phylum Chordata is the most important one for the comparative psychologist. Its members are described below:

Phylum: Chordata

Subphyla:	Vertebrata Cephalochordata Urochordata
Classes of vertebrata:	Mammalia Aves[1] Reptilia Amphibia Osteichthyes[2] Chondrichthyes[3] Agnatha Placodermi
Subclasses of mammalia:	Theria[4] Prototheria[5]

[1] Birds.
[2] Includes body fishes.
[3] Includes sharks.
[4] Viviparous mammals.
[5] Egg-laying mammals.

Orders of theria:	
	Marsupialia (e.g., possum, kangaroo)
	Insectivora (mole, shrew)
	Dermoptera (flying lemur)
	Chiroptera (bat)
	Edentata (sloth)
	Pholidota (pangolin)
	Primates (other lemurs, monkey, man)
	Rodentia (rat, beaver)
	Lagomorpha (hare, rabbit)
	Cetacea (whale, dolphin)
	Carnivora (cat, dog)
	Tubulidentata (aardvark)
	Proboscidea (elephant)
	Hyracoidea (cony)
	Sirenia (sea cow)
	Perissodactyla (horse, rhinoceros)
	Artiodactyla (pig, cow, deer)

It is important to remember when working with this zoological taxonomy that it is continually changing. Taxonomists identify and classify species and reorganize their schema as a result of new discoveries. Improved techniques for identifying species and assessing the degree of resemblance between species also lead to reorganization of the schema. Zoologists frequently differ in their opinion about the correctness of a particular classification. At any given time, however, zoological taxonomy provides a convenient schema for us to use.

Before leaving this discussion of zoological taxonomy, we should look briefly at the kinds of information zoologists use to assist them in assigning species to their place in the hierarchical taxonomy.

The Bases for Taxonomic Classifications

What kinds of data do taxonomists use to help them decide on the classification of a new species?

1. The major source of data has been from morphological

studies, in which the anatomical features of different species are examined. In general, the greater the similarity, the more closely are the two species related (although many exceptions to this rule could be enumerated). Morphological studies are used so often because they are the easist to conduct. Animals can be easily collected, preserved, and stored.

2. The study of embryology (the development of the animal from egg to adult) has also been used, for early stages in the development of an animal often reveal relationships that are no longer apparent when the adult animals are studied.

3. In a similar manner, physical characteristics such as the structure of the nervous system or the composition of the blood plasma provide clues to relationships between species.

4. Paleontology provides usable data from the cataloging and description of fossils of extinct animals. These extinct species often provide intermediate connections between species, which enables the taxonomist to infer the manner in which a newly discovered species developed. Of course, many species do not possess structures that can be fossilized; thus many extinct species cannot be studied. The paleontologist himself has a difficult task in classifying a newly discovered, extinct species. The only data he can use involve a morphological study of the remains and comparison with a core of paleontological data.

5. The distribution of animals over a locale (zoogeography) can also be used to provide clues to the relationship of species, especially if educated guesses can be made as to the migration of species in the past.

6. The study of animal behavior is being used more and more today to establish the existence of closely related species. For example, the study of courtship behavior and the noises animals make (birds singing, crickets chirping, frogs croaking) has been used to determine the number of species in some similar groups of animals.

7. The final and most basic source of data used by the taxonomist is genetic research. Of course, genetic differences underlie the other bases of taxonomy. Relationships between

species are determined by the extent of their shared genetic factors. Although genetics is the basis of taxonomy, genetic studies are rarely used to provide the taxonomist with useful data because of the difficulties and time involved in carrying out such studies.

Morphological studies are the easiest source of data for the taxonomist and were first used historically. Paleontological studies require the existence and locating of fossil remains, and the remaining sources require capturing and preserving live specimens. Accurate classification, however, requires the use and weighing of data from all of these sources.

The Concept of Race

It is interesting, in light of the information above, to examine the concept of race as it applies to man. According to the 1950 UNESCO Statement on Race by Social Scientists (Montagu 1963), all men belong to the same species, *Homo sapiens*, and it is most likely that all men derived from the same common ancestor. Differences between groups of men are probably due to the operation of evolutionary factors of differentiation (such as isolation). The total population of men contains different groups which differ in the frequency of one or more genes. These groups, which are called *races*, are capable of interbreeding, but because of past barriers, they have developed independently and so exhibit different physical attributes. The UNESCO Statement pointed out that national, religious, geographic, linguistic, or cultural groups are not necessarily races. Thus Jews, Frenchmen, or those who speak Spanish are not a race. Three major races were distinguished in the Statement—mongoloid, negroid, and caucasoid. The existence of other races (such as the aboriginal inhabitants of Australia) has been postulated. There is disagreement about the exact number of races. In fact, "race" is a terminological convenience rather than a concept that can be operationally *and* usefully defined. The UNESCO Statement notes that mental characteristics, temperament, and personality do not appear to vary with race as far as present evidence allows us to determine; they are determined by cultural experiences and not by inborn genetic differences.

The concept of *race* is similar to the concept of a subspecies. While it seems clear that all men are physically capable of interbreeding, they differ from other animals in the plasticity of their behavior and their adaptability. Human mating is determined to a large extent by learned factors. The low rate of human racial interbreeding results from learning, whereas, in contrast, the failure of two groups of, say, finches to interbreed occurs because of differing, genetically determined courtship patterns.

The UNESCO Statement emphasizes that there is no evidence that races differ in psychological traits. (Neither is there evidence that they do *not* differ.) Psychological measures are notoriously crude. It is no wonder that they fail to detect reliable and valid differences between different groups. Since the different races or subspecies of man differ in physical traits, it seems highly likely that they will differ in other respects too. To accept this possibility is not to argue that one race is inferior to another, it simply means that races, just as individuals, may differ from one another.

Although it is difficult to exclude emotions and politics from science, the advance of knowledge can be impeded by their inclusion. It is said in Europe that research conducted in the United States on questions such as the above is to be distrusted. The data are likely to be distorted. Belief in genetic determination favors those who support the status quo, whereas a belief in environmental influences suits those who are working for racial and sexual equality. If this contention is true, then the answers to particular questions concerning individual cultural and racial differences may be unavailable for many decades.

17

References

Mayr, E. 1969. *Principles of systematic zoology*. New York: McGraw-Hill.

Montagu, A. 1963. *Race, science, and humanity*. New York: Van Nostrand Reinhold.

Villee, C.A.; Walker, W.F.; and Smith, F.E. 1963. *General zoology*. Philadelphia: Saunders.

Waters, R.H.; Rethlingshafer, D.A.; and Caldwell, W.E. 1960. *Principles of comparative psychology*. New York: McGraw-Hill.

Chapter 3

The Evolution of Animals

A BASIC PROBLEM in comparative psychology lies in the way the behavior of a particular animal evolved from primitive ancestors (now extinct), through mediating species (also now extinct), until the behavior of the contemporary species was reached. Some knowledge of the principles of evolution is therefore needed in order to cope with this major problem.

Taxonomic Classification and Evolution

In the discussion of taxonomy in Chapter 2, there are many implicit references to evolution but no specific discussion. A good taxonomy has many uses, even in the absence of evolutionary implications. In any science, accurate description and definition of the objects to be studied generally precede a meaningful analysis and study of the objects. In addition, a good taxonomy makes for economy of description. But convenience is not the only criterion for judging the merits of a taxonomy.

A taxonomic classification is also an attempt to describe the degree of similarity between different species. One species of a particular genus is not only considered to be more similar to other species in the same genus than to those in another genus, but the species in one genus are also considered to have evolved from an original, common ancestor. Each category (genus, family, order, class, and phylum) is considered to constitute an evolutionary unit as well as a taxonomic unit.

For many reasons, taxonomy can never indicate evolutionary trends exactly. Evolution appears to be a continuous process, whereas taxonomy imposes boundaries between species. Taxonomy also fails to include the time element involved in the evolutionary process. In addition, a taxonomy is firmly rooted in empirical data, whereas evolutionary relationships can be inferred only from available evidence.

Mayr (1969) claims that reconstruction of the evolution of the species (the phylogeny of the species) and taxonomic classification are based on the same raw data (the comparison of different species and an assessment of their similarities and differences), but phylogeny is not based on taxonomy, nor vice versa.* However, a classification that is consistent with the evolutionary development of different species stands a better chance of being a satisfactory taxonomy, for taxonomic units that coincide with evolutionary groups are likely to share many characteristics.

Furthermore, the evolution of species provides the intellectual justification for the science of taxonomy. Taxonomic groups do not exist as arbitrary products of the human mind. Natural groups exist because the members of such groups are descended from common ancestors. Thus evolution can provide a rationale for the existence of taxonomic groups.

What Is Evolution?

Evolution is the process that has been postulated in order

---

* The study of the evolutionary relationships among animals is known as *systematic zoology.*

to account for the appearance on the earth today of many millions of species of animals. According to this view, all species of animals are descended from precellular aggregates of organic molecules which existed in the oceans and waters of the earth millions of years ago. How is evolution thought to operate?

Evolution was described in simple terms by Charles Darwin as "descent with modification." This phrase is now believed to incorporate two essential processes: variation in genetic composition of a population, and the modification of this variation by natural selection.

The origin of variation is found in a variety of genetic processes. In rare circumstances new genetic combinations can occur through mutation. More often, though, the genes may be "shuffled" by genetic recombination (through bisexual mating), so that new combinations are available for natural selection to work on.

When a population of animals has genetic variability, natural selection can operate. The basic process outlined by Darwin is as follows. When conditions permit the survival of all offspring, the number of animals in a population tends to rise geometrically. Factors such as the availability of food, however, seldom permit a population to increase unchecked. Thus there arises a competition, or struggle for survival, among the members of the population. The genetic variation among the members of the population means that some members are more fitted for survival; in this struggle for survival, only the fittest live to reproduce.

Note that "fittest," in this context, does *not* mean the healthiest or the strongest. It means those individuals who possess characteristics that enable them to live and produce relatively more viable offspring. This selection process means that the genetic composition of the population changes, for the less fit do not live to contribute to the gene pool of the next generation.

Although chance is responsible for the origin of gene mutations and the various ways in which these mutations are juggled in the genetic structure, the perpetuation of the genetic changes is determined by their success in nature. Thus there are two factors that affect natural selection:

1. Selection by internal characteristics. The new organisms may be less able to reproduce, sometimes to the point of being sterile. Ross (1966) reports that attempts to breed chickens selectively so that they had long legs produced animals with reduced reproductive capacity.

2. Selection by environment. A famous example is that of the giraffe. In times of food shortage, those members of the population with longer necks were able to reach food more easily and thus were more likely to survive.

Often both factors can operate. In certain populations of African Negroes, sickle cell anemia is common. When a person inherits the genetic factor responsible for the disease from both parents, he may develop anemia and die. (This person is not a viable organism.) However, if he inherits the genetic factors responsible for normal cell development from both parents, he may easily succumb to malaria, for the genetic factor responsible for sickle cell anemia also increases resistance to malaria. Those who inherit the genetic factor for sickle cell anemia from one parent and the genetic factor responsible for normal cells from the other parent are more likely to survive.

Evolutionary Adaptation And Speciation

There are two major kinds of evolution, *evolutionary adaptation* and *speciation*. Evolutionary adaptation occurs when the environmental factors determining natural selection remain fairly constant, and the entire species tends to become better adapted to the environment. If the environment changes gradually, the entire species may change with it. Over a long period of time, therefore, the population can change, so that its members at different times constitute different species.

Evolutionary changes can move toward the stability of the existing organism (centripetal selection) or away from it (centrifugal selection). If an organism is well adapted to its environment, and if the environment stays about the same, modifications of the organism most likely will cause it to be less well adapted to its environment and so be less likely to survive. Many lineages seem to have changed very little over time; for example, the possum (*Didelphis virginicus*) is remarkably similar to its Cretaceous ancestor of 100 million years ago. In centrifugal selection the organism changes drastically over time. Two factors affect the rate of change: the rate of advantageous mutations and the intensity of selection pressures.

Speciation occurs when two different populations of a species become isolated in some way and are subject to different environmental influences. They evolve differently and their characteristics diverge. Eventually the two populations constitute two different species.

The effect of evolution is not only to change the phenotypes (observable characteristics) of animals, but also to change the number of species of animals (and, in general over the past million years, to increase the number of species). There are several ways in which the number of species can grow. Essentially, all of them involve isolating one group of a population from another group. Once this is achieved, the two groups can evolve independently of one another and so develop into two different species.

If we consider bisexual species only, the principal isolating factors are:

1. *Geographical isolation*. Two groups of the population come to occupy a divided, or disjunct, territory in which no genetic interchange can take place between the two populations.

2. *Range isolation*. The two groups of the population

occupy the same region but dwell in different habitats. Among the deer mice, *Peromyscus maniculatus* occupies prairie areas, while *Peromyscus leucopus* occupies woods and forests.

3. *Host isolation*. This is relevant for parasites. For example, a species of the North American silkworm moth, which feeds only on larch trees, arose from a species that fed on angiosperm trees.

4. *Isolation by seasonal timing*. Two populations may become isolated by seasonal timing, as in the case of two species of the North American field cricket (*Acheta*), which occupy the same territory but mature at different times (one in the spring and one in the autumn).

5. *Behavioral isolation*. Two populations of flies may be prevented from interbreeding simply by the fact that one group is active in daylight, the other only at dawn and at dusk.

These factors lead to isolation of a group and thus to speciation.

An Example of Phylogenetic Explanation

Colbert (1958) has described the evolution (or phylogenesis) of some behaviors that will illustrate the process we are discussing here. One interesting example concerns an explanation of the behavior of modern species of cats and dogs, using a study of their morphological evolution.

Cats and dogs differ considerably. Dogs are friendly, sociable, and easily trained. They like to live with men and to work for men. They are cooperative. Cats, on the other hand, are friendly but not sociable. They like to live with men but primarily for the food and protection such association provides for them. They are independent and, though trainable, cannot be used for work or play. While the dog is a truly domesticated animal, the cat is essentially a wild animal that tolerates (and is tolerated by) man.

All modern carnivores had their source in a carnivore family known as the Miacidae in Eocene times. They were about the size of house cats and lived in forests. Their teeth were adapted to eating fresh meat. They had small, nipping incisor teeth in the front for biting; large, dagger canine teeth for stabbing and killing; and in the side of the mouth were teeth for cutting, working much like shearing blades. These early miacids were similar to some of the Old World civets such as the Mediterranean genet.

By Oligocene times, the canids and the felids had diverged. The canids pursued prey. They were good runners and were adapted to catching and holding their prey while on the run. They also developed a cooperative system of hunting in which they shared the burden of catching prey. Canids were generalized carnivores; they ate carrion and even vegetables. Their back teeth were blunt enough to be used for crushing food.

The felids, in contrast, emphasized the lone hunt and ambush of prey. They were powerful, supple animals, good at climbing. Their running strength lay in being able to run very fast for short distances rather than in having stamina for long chases. Their claws were suitable for grasping and tearing prey, while they used their teeth for stabbing and shearing. They ate meat and nothing else.

The two types evolved at different rates. The felids reached a high degree of specialization early in their evolutionary development, while the canids evolved slowly.

Colbert argues that the dog is plastic in its behavior because it is relatively unspecialized physically. It is highly intelligent and social and can adapt to man's needs, especially if selectively bred. The cat, on the other hand, is fixed in its behavior because it has evolved into a highly specialized animal. It is intelligent but has a long history of being nonsocial. Its inflexibility prevents it from sharing human ways as dogs do, and since it did not evolve from a pack animal, it never regards a human as a master or "leader of the pack."

25

Phylogenesis and Comparative Psychology

If we are interested in the phylogenesis of behavior, we obviously cannot study the ancestors of present-day species in the laboratory, because they no longer survive. Two options remain open to us. First, we can identify current species, which resemble ancestral animals, and study them. For example, in this chapter the possum and the genet have been described as being similar to extinct species and as having evolved very little. Some of these species may resemble animals that are directly ancestral to current species, as the genet resembles the miacids that evolved into the felids and canids. If we could identify enough such species, we could attempt to observe the phylogenesis of behavior (see Table 3.1).

This approach would necessitate the assumption that morphology is a good index of behavior. The genet may resemble fossil records of miacids morphologically, but we do not know that it resembled them in behavior. It may be argued that the teeth were similar and the habitats identical, but comparative psychologists usually do not study the mode of tearing and chewing food; they investigate such behaviors as maze-running, color vision, and visual cliff performance. In these aspects of behavior, similar morphologies are no guarantee of similar performance.

A second approach is to study the fossil records of early animals. If an adequate reconstruction of phylogenies is possible, then we can perhaps infer differences in behavior from the morphology of the fossil records and compare ancestral species to current species. But this approach relies even more heavily than the former on the identity between morphology and behavior. Again, this may suffice for the biologist, but is grossly inadequate for the comparative psychologist.

Should you doubt that morphology is a poor guide to behavior studied by psychologists, consider man. Most men would leave similar fossil records, but the behavior of different men varies widely. Brain and mental abilities do not leave a fossil record.

TABLE 3.1
Suggested family tree for some of the commoner groups of vertebrates.
After Ross, (1966, p. 75.)

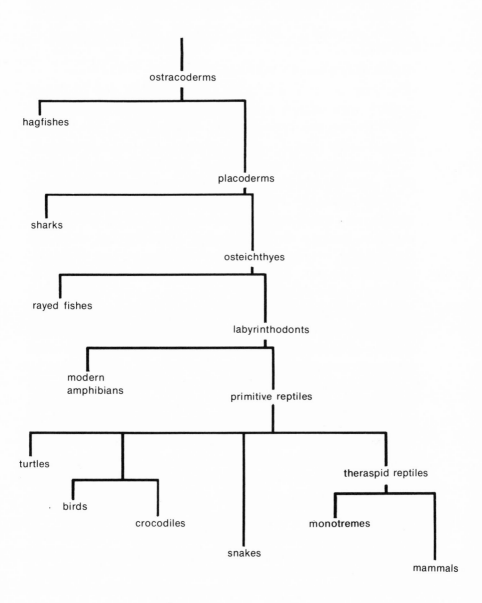

It is for these reasons that this book is subtitled "phyletic differences in behavior." This task of describing phylogenetic differences in behavior is possible, but for the time being, it is an open question. We will return to this problem in Chapter 13.

Phylogeny and Ontogeny

It is often said that ontogeny recapitulates phylogeny (the law of recapitulation). What this means is that the course of development of an embryo resembles the evolutionary development of the embryo once it is born. Documentation of the theory, though, is hard to obtain. Applied to behavior rather than physical structure, this idea means that the course of development of a behavior in a human infant resembles the sequence in which the behavior evolved in the human species.

Conceptual Parallels

A comparison of phylogeny and ontogeny can be made at the conceptual level. Gilbert (1970) has illustrated this approach, noting, first, that there are four precepts in the law of natural selection (or theory of evolution): (1) survival of a particular characteristic of an animal is related to the contribution of that characteristic to the relative fertility of the animal; (2) the existence of any characteristic in an animal is the result of a history of selection for fertility in the animal's ancestors; (3) the only mechanisms that need be invoked to account for a particular phylogeny are those mechanisms related to the variation of characters and to the selection of varieties by the environment; (4) phylogeny is continuous.

To parallel this analysis, Gilbert noted that a psychologist looking at ontogeny from a learning viewpoint would propose four similar precepts for behavioral development: (1) survival

28

of a particular response in the repertoire of an animal is related to the relative frequency with which reinforcement follows the appearance of the response; (2) the existence of a particular response in the repertoire of the animal is the result of the reinforcement history of the animal with respect to that particular response; (3) the only mechanisms that need be invoked to account for a particular ontogeny are those related to variation in responses and to selection of varieties by the environment; (4) ontogeny is continuous.

Ontogenetic contingencies are limited by phylogenetic contingencies. For example, the fact that behavior varies and is reinforceable depends on the phylogenetic history of the animal. Similarly, the effectiveness of phylogenetic contingencies depends on ontogenetic contingencies (monkeys, given a particular history of reinforcement, do not mate satisfactorily).

Although the parallel is not perfect, Gilbert noted how close it can be. In the change that took place in the peppered moth in England during the Industrial Revolution (the darker members of the species became increasingly common [see Kettlewell 1961]), the following sequence of events took place:

1. The environment became sootier.
2. The phenotypes present included a variety of shades of moths, from very light to very dark.
3. An agent of selection was at work; robins, or hedge-sparrows, ate lighter-colored moths because they were more visible against a sooty background.
4. As a result, the members of successive generations became darker, since only the dark moths lived to reproduce.

For the development of speech in human infants we have a similar sequence of events:

1. Environment—parents who speak English
2. Repertoire—a variety of vocal sounds made by infant

3. Agent of selection—parents respond socially to sounds
   made by infant, which resemble English
4. Result—infant learns to speak English

Skinner also noted the similarity between phylogeny and ontogeny (Skinner 1966), but pointed to some differences between the two phenomena. He noted that the contingencies responsible for the natural selection of species characteristics were in effect long ago. Thus the process remains an inference, whereas ontogenetic hypotheses can be put to the test. When we see a rat press a bar (or even hear a baby speak), we can examine a history of the contingencies that led to this particular behavior, but when we see a spider spin a web we can record no comparable history. Skinner warned against making mistaken inferences on the basis of the parallel between ontogeny and phylogeny.

Skinner noted that phylogenetic contingencies can interfere with ontogenetic ones. For example, a pig trained by Breland and Breland (1966) to carry coins to a piggy bank and deposit them would stop along the way to drop the coins, root them, and toss them in the air. Ontogenetic contingencies can also suppress phylogenetic activities. When Skinner trained pigeons to peck keys in response to certain stimuli he could arrange the reinforcement contingencies so that the pigeon would peck the keys rapidly and thus fail to eat the grain which was the reinforcer.

Empirical Parallels

Ontogenetic development may empirically resemble the phylogenetic development of behavior. For example, in Chapter 10 ("Social Behavior"), we note Hebb's and Thompson's (1969) argument that the ontogenetic development of emotion resembles the phylogenetic development and that in both cases the trend is toward greater emotionality. A similar argument can be made for learning. Just as there is some doubt that the most primitive species of animals can be conditioned, so is there doubt that human fetuses and babies younger than six weeks can be conditioned (Gray 1966). A parallel is sometimes drawn for the embryonic development of the human fetus; it is asserted that at different stages of development the human embryo resembles the embryo form of successively more phylogenetically advanced species.

Despite these simple parallels there has been no detailed analysis of particular behavior, from both an ontogenetic or a phylogenetic perspective. Analysis has remained at a simple level, almost at an armchair perspective. It *looks* as if there is a similarity, but so far we have been unable to test empirically whether there is. This being the case, the parallel must be considered intriguing but unproven.

References

Breland, K.; and Breland, M. 1966. *Animal behavior*. New York: Macmillan.

Colbert, E.H. 1958. Morphology and behavior. In *Behavior and evolution,* ed. A. Roe and G.G. Simpson, pp. 27-47. New Haven: Yale Univ. Press.

Gilbert, R.M. 1970. Psychology and biology. *Canadian Psychologist* 11:221-38.

Gray, P.H. 1966. *The comparative analysis of behavior*. Dubuque, Iowa: Brown.

Hebb, D.O.; and Thompson, W.R. 1969. The social significance of animal studies. In *The handbook of social psychology,* ed. G. Lindzey and E. Aronson, vol. 2, pp. 729-74. Reading, Mass.: Addison-Wesley.

Kettlewell, H.B.D. 1961. The phenomenon of industrial melanism in Lepidoptera. *Annual Review of Entomology* 6:245-62.

Mayr, E. 1969. *Principles of systematic zoology*. New York: McGraw-Hill.

Ross, H.H. 1966. *Understanding evolution*. Englewood Cliffs, N.J.: Prentice-Hall.

Skinner, B.F. 1966. The phylogeny and ontogeny of behavior. *Science* 153:1,205-13.

31

II
Anatomical and
Physiological Differences

Chapter 4

The Influence of Size and Structure

THE SIZE AND STRUCTURE of an animal obviously affect its behavior significantly. Behavioral differences between two species can result from these basic anatomical differences. The development of prehensile tails and limbs in a primate enables the animal to engage in more complex manipulative behavior than animals without these structures.

However, a mere catalogue of differences in the structures of various animals would not be very instructive. We need to find differences that have more general relevance to the comparative psychologist. The first difference to be noted is the importance of the size of the animal.

Size

Went (1968) argues that the emergence of man as a creature with a highly developed technology from among the millions of animal species is attributable not only to his brain volume, his upright posture, his highly developed hands, and his use of fire, as other writers have suggested, but also to his size.

The size of an animal has important consequences for its physiological and mechanical systems. Animals are composed of a collection of cells which are roughly the same size in all animals. This means that different sizes of animals is due almost exclusively to the different number of cells they contain.

Let us consider how chemicals are transmitted from one location to another in animals. In cells this transmission takes place by the process of diffusion. Molecules of sugar, for example, become evenly distributed within a cell in a matter of seconds after their introduction. If distribution of sugar in man depended on diffusion, it would take too long for sugar to diffuse from his stomach to his feet and hands. Therefore, in an animal appreciably larger than one cell, some kind of hydraulic "streaming" is necessary in order for chemicals to be distributed throughout the organism. Went noted that almost without exception animals larger than one millimeter have a heart or some other organ responsible for the circulation of chemicals throughout the animal.

To take another example, if an animal had to rely on diffusion to obtain oxygen for its tissues, there would be a limit on its size. Larger animals have therefore developed lungs or gills to provide oxygen.

Went noted that social insects are highly specialized, with fairly complex societies, as is illustrated by ants. Yet ants have never developed a technology and dominated the earth the way humans do. (They do, of course, dominate their own niche.) Why? Are there reasons other than size or complexity of the nervous system?

1. It can easily be shown that an animal the size of an ant could never use fire. A flame must be larger than a few millimeters in length in order for it to be stable. If the flame is to be nourished by solid combustible material, the burning pieces have to be surrounded by other pieces of combustible material. An ant could never drag large enough pieces of wood to a fire, place them close enough to it, or stay close enough to the fire to benefit from the heat.

2. The size of an animal has important consequences for its behavior. For example, for an animal the size of man, gravitational forces are much stronger than molecular adhesive forces and electrostatic forces, whereas, for animals the size of an ant, adhesive and electrostatic forces are much stronger than gravitational forces. This is why an ant can walk up a vertical surface and a man cannot. However, an ant also sticks more easily to other particles. Friction is dangerous for the ant, for if it became electrostatically charged it would be dominated by electrostatic forces.

To be sure, gravitational forces have their disadvantages. Consider what happens when an animal falls over. The kinetic energy developed when a man falls over is some 20 to 100 times that of a child who falls. The greater the kinetic energy, the greater the chance the animal will break a bone in the fall. Thus children rarely break bones when they trip, but adults frequently do. If men were twice as tall as they are, it would not be safe for them to walk upright. Land animals larger than man always have four legs to give them greater stability. A leafcutter ant, on the other hand, can cut off a piece of leaf high in a tree and fall 50 feet to the ground without being hurt.

3. The size of an animal has implications for the power with which it can wield tools. A club that could kill an animal could not be swung effectively by a child. Neither could a child throw a spear or shoot an arrow with sufficient momentum to kill. Similar limitations affect the use of axes, chisels, and hammers. If men were only three feet tall, they could not cut timber or excavate a mine in solid rock. The existence of gnomes is a practical impossibility.

Went has argued persuasively that an animal that could develop a world-dominating technology would have to be roughly the size of man. Some of his arguments, however, are based on the assumption that any dominating animal would have to use the same methods and the same technology. For example, it may take a man six feet tall to effectively club a large animal to death, but even an ant could poison a large animal, given a sufficiently strong venom. In spite of this one criticism of Went's thesis, the life of a large animal is surely very different from the life of a small one. A definite discontinuity exists between the microscopic and the macroscopic worlds. An animal's behavior is to a considerable extent determined by its size.

Structure: Radial and Bilateral Symmetry

An important difference in animals is that of anatomical symmetry. The simplest animals are the Protozoa, which are single cells of changing shapes. The next step in structural complexity comes with organisms that consist of many cells in a loose association, such as the Porifera (sponges). The first animals to show a closely integrated association in their cellular makeup are the Coelenterata (polyps and medusae) and the Echinodermata (includes the starfish), which are radially symmetrical (see Fig. 4.1). The flatworm of the phylum Platyhelminthes is an example of a primitive, bilaterally symmetrical animal (see Fig. 4.2).

Maier and Schneirla (1964) have argued that radial symmetry is a more primitive structural pattern than bilateral symmetry insofar as its importance for behavior is concerned. Radially symmetrical animals can move in the direction of the principal axis of symmetry (with the top of the animal forward, as in the medusae) or at right angles to this axis, as in the starfish. Maier and Schneirla considered bilateral symmetry to be an advance over radial symmetry, because the former allows for much better orientation and much more efficient locomotion.

Typically, radially symmetrical animals have developed no more than radially symmetrical nerve nets, whereas bilaterally symmetrical animals have developed centralized nervous systems. It is not clear whether this is necessarily tied to the symmetry of the animal. It is conceivable that a radially

FIGURE 4.1.
The five living classes of the Echinodermata, all of which are radially symmetrical. From Villee et al., 1963, p. 339.

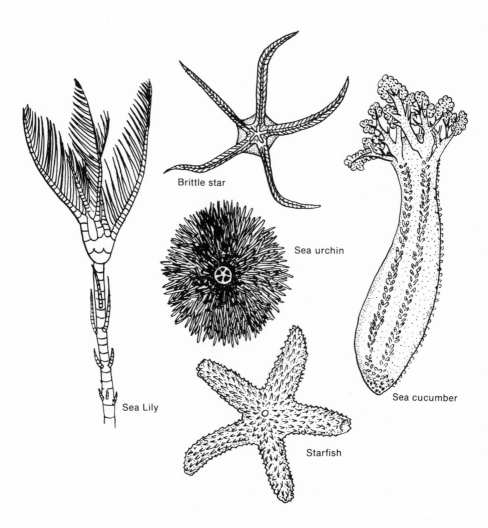

Brittle star

Sea urchin

Sea Lily

Starfish

Sea cucumber

FIGURE 4.2.
A bilaterally symmetrical animal, the flatworm, genus Dugesia. From
Villee et al., 1963, p. 197.

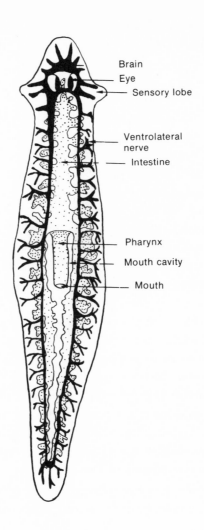

symmetrical animal could develop a centralized lump of nervous tissue which could have evolved into a complex mechanism, as in bilaterally symmetrical animals. This has not occurred, however.

It *is* clear that bilateral symmetry allows for the development of specialized organs such as a head and tail and that with these specialized organs there have developed more complex forms of behavior.

Polymorphs

There are many species of animals that possess several morphological types.* All nonhermaphroditic species have, by definition, both male and female members. In addition, the morphological characteristics of a species can vary with such factors as age, climate, and diet.

Above and beyond these variations, some species have developed grossly different morphological types, called polymorphs. Ants, termites, and bees are examples of such differentiation. An ant colony may contain a queen, males, and three types of sterile females—workers, soldiers, and honey ants. The development of these different types is determined by the nutriment fed to the larvae, whether the egg is fertilized or not, and by age.

Polymorphic forms (Fig. 4.3) are merely more extreme examples of the typical morphological changes that many species show. However, ants, termites, and bees (all from the phylum Arthropoda) are unique in the extreme development of polymorphic forms and in the orchestration of these forms in the functioning of the colony.

The importance of polymorphic forms to the comparative psychologist lies in the fact that the different polymorphs per-

*Several subtypes with differing structures.

form different tasks in their colonies. In the bee, where the polymorphs are a result of aging, the newly hatched worker bee first cleans out newly vacated cells. After a few days the salivary glands begin to secrete royal jelly and the worker bee becomes a nurse, feeding the larvae. After about 10 days of this the salivary glands begin to stop producing the royal jelly, and the wax glands begin to function. Now the bee begins to build honeycombs. This continues for about three weeks, after which the wax glands cease functioning; the

FIGURE 4.3
The polymorphs of the ant. From Villee et al., 1963, p. 323.

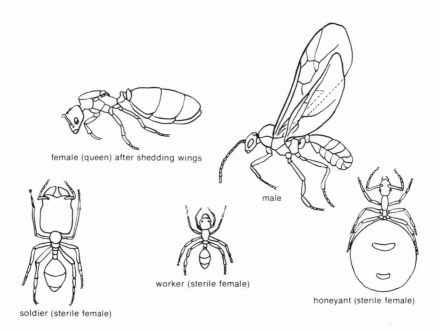

female (queen) after shedding wings

male

worker (sterile female)

honeyant (sterile female)

soldier (sterile female)

remaining four or five weeks of life are spent foraging for pollen and nectar.*

Metamorphosis

Metamorphosis is a change in the shape or relative size of body parts during the growth of an animal. In many animals, such as the mammals, the young closely resemble the adults, so little metamorphosis takes place. In other species there is marked metamorphosis. For example, *Gonionemus,* a genus of small medusae (phylum Coelenterata) first develops from the egg into a small ciliated larva, the planula. This planula attaches itself to a solid object and eventually becomes a polyp. Metamorphosis occurs in the phylum Arthropoda, as is illustrated by the butterflies with their larval stage as caterpillars. Metamorphosis also takes place in the phylum Chordata, as is illustrated by the development of the frog from the egg via the intermediate stage of the tadpole.

Metamorphosis is a kind of delayed embryonic development which in some species takes place while the organism is still in the egg or placental stage. In other species metamorphosis is not marked because of the simplicity of the organism (as in the phylum Protozoa) or because the young resemble the adult upon hatching, as is illustrated in the phylum Arthropoda by the silverfish.

There appears to be little pattern in the presence or absence (or the extent) of metamorphosis throughout phyla. But in more developed and complex animals such as mammals, metamorphosis is minimal and the embryo develops extensively while in the womb. It is interesting that the period of embryonic development is longer in the higher animals than in the lower.

---

* The time at which these changes in function occur vary, of course, from individual to individual and are also affected by such factors as the hive conditions.

The behavioral effects of metamorphosis are not well documented, but they undoubtedly exist. For example, tropisms (tendencies to move or to orient to physical and chemical stimuli, such as the tendency of some organisms to move toward or away from bright light sources) may differ in the larva and the adult insect. In a later chapter we will review some of the differences in the learning behavior of different species. It would be interesting to investigate learning behavior in both the larval and the adult stage of different species. Perhaps the level of functioning is different in the two stages. To our knowledge, this has not yet been studied.

Conclusion

I have tried to illustrate in this chapter how the size and structure of an animal can influence its behavior. A few simple structural changes that are associated with the animal's position on the phyletic scale (such as bilateral symmetry) were noted.

It is probably true, however, that psychologists have not been especially interested in the influence of size and structure as it is discussed here. Instead, they focus more on the nervous systems of different species, since the behavior of animals is closely tied to the structure and complexity of their nervous systems. Furthermore, the changes in the nervous system associated with the position of the animal on the phyletic scale are easier to identify and easier to relate to behavioral changes. In the next two chapters we will explore some phyletic differences and trends in the nervous system of different animals—in the peripheral nervous system, the sense organs, and the central nervous system.

References

Maier, N.R.F.; and Schneirla, T.C. 1964. *Principles of animal psychology*. New York: Dover.

Villee, C.A.; Walker, W.F.; and Smith, F.E. 1963. *General zoology*. Philadelphia: Saunders.

Went, F.W. 1968. The size of man. *American Scientist* 56:400-13.

Chapter 5

The Nervous System

THE BEHAVIOR OF animals is largely determined by their nervous systems. Phyletic differences in behavior, therefore, must depend largely on phyletic differences in the nervous system.

My aim in this chapter is not to detail the different neural mechanisms that are responsible for the appearance of particular behaviors of particular species. Such a task is beyond the scope of this book; furthermore, to do so would leave us with a mass of data from which it would be difficult to identify phyletic trends. (Perhaps it should be added that knowledge of neural mechanisms in the control of behavior is far from complete, so the data would be only a small part of what may eventually be known.) What I will try to do instead is discuss two general phyletic trends in the structure of the nervous system and explore their implications for the behavior of animals. The examples chosen for discussion should illustrate the kinds of analyses that can be undertaken when correlating properties of the nervous system with aspects of behavior.

General Phyletic Trends

As Tavolga (1969) has noted, the simplest organisms are unicellular; the entire organism is at the same time a receptor, conductor, effector, and integrator. In multicellular animals, neural cells appear and can be classified into three types on the basis of their function: receptors, transmitters, and effectors.

In the radially symmetrical coelenterate, *Hydra,* neural cells are arranged in a nerve net; there is no centralization of the net, though some portions of the animal may have greater concentrations of neural cells than others.

Two developments are noticeable in the Echinodermata (for example, the sea urchin). The neural cells (ganglia) are organized into a number of main tracts, and association neurons appear. The latter are neural cells which interconnect with other neural cells, thus allowing a multiplicity of neural processes. These more complex nervous systems are still uncentralized. Tavolga notes that animals with diffuse nervous systems tend to be sessile, or slow-moving. They rarely pursue prey, preferring, instead, to wait for their prey to blunder along, or else to encounter food during their slow wanderings.

The advent of bilateral symmetry in animals is associated with the development of a permanent, specialized head end, a development known as cephalization. In the flatworm, *Planaria,* there is a primitive head which acts to some extent as an integrating mechanism. In these primitive, bilaterally symmetrical invertebrates there are often subsidiary concentrations of neural cells. The apex of this form of nervous system is found in the Arthropoda, where there is much consolidation into ganglia.

In the vertebrates, brain size (cephalization) is more advanced. The development that seems to be more important for species differentiation among the vertebrates is the growth of cortical control, which will be described later.

48

The Influence of Brain Size

Rensch (1956) noted that many lines of descent show a successive increase of body size, hence an increase in the *absolute* size of the brain. This trend is especially true of mammals. (On the other hand, the *relative* brain size decreases as the size of the typical species member increases.) Rensch phrased his observation in terms of phylogenesis, but we may take the observation and apply it to the phyletic scale as defined in Chapter 1.

Within the central nervous system there is often an increase in the relative size of particular structures in species higher in the phyletic scale. This rule of progression applies to the *corpora pedunculata* in insects and to the forebrain in higher vertebrates. The progression is found for the quantity of neurons, as well as their arrangement and properties. The neurons become more densely arranged, forming more specialized centers. In general, sensory neurons remain small, but there are more of them. Rensch felt that this development facilitated the perception of complex stimuli. Motor neurons generally become larger, which possibly facilitates the conduction of motor excitation, thus improving responses.

Rensch has conducted a number of studies exploring the influence of absolute brain size on the ability to learn. (Unfortunately, he does not seem to have controlled for absolute body size in his early studies.) Among the insects, those with large brains appear to have more complicated *copora pedunculata,* a characteristic which seems to be associated with the complexity of behavior. Rensch noted that the larger wasps and bees in Europe (families Vespidae and Apidae) had more complicated social behaviors than the smaller species. Similarly, the social ants have larger brains than the ants which show little social behavior. Rensch determined that there were no data available to enable him to decide whether the learning capability of insects was related to their brain size.

Rensch felt that in the vertebrates, brain size was related to learning capabilities. He noted that courtship was more "complicated" in large species of grouse, for example, than in small species. In more controlled studies of domestic fowl, large species were found to be able to master more visual tasks involving discrimination (simultaneously, it seems) than were smaller species. In a series of learning studies, rats mastered tasks faster than mice and were capable of learning more tasks.

Rensch initiated some studies of learning in the largest terrestrial mammal, the elephant. The brain of this mammal weighs around 6,000 grams, compared to man's 1,350-gram brain. A young Indian elephant was trained to discriminate between pairs of patterns. As soon as she mastered one pair, she was trained on the next. Eventually the elephant was able to recognize and respond correctly to 40 different patterns. Rensch also noted that in India, elephants 20 to 30 years old can respond to over 20 different commands.

Rensch also found that large animals can retain information for longer periods of time than can smaller animals. In the fish family, Cyprinodontidae, large species (such as the Mexican swordtail, *Xiphophorus helleri*) retained learned discriminations for much longer than did small species (such as the guppy, *Lebistes reticulatus*). Similarly, rats retain learned discriminations longer than do mice. Rensch's elephant could remember 12 of 13 discrimination tasks (that is, she performed significantly better than mere chance would account for) after one year without training. Perhaps an elephant indeed never forgets!

Related to the observations of Rensch are the data reported by Jerison (1970) on the brain size of different ungulates (animals with hooves) and carnivores during different epochs of fossil history. Jerison concluded that there has been a progressive increase in the relative brain size of animals, accompanied by increased diversity in existing, relative brain sizes. Every epoch has seen the evolution of some small-brained species, but large-brained species have more frequently developed in relatively recent epochs.

Corticalization of Function

In addition to the brain growing in size during fossil history (and over the phyletic scale), there has been an accompanying growth in the relative size of the cortex. There appears to be a shifting of functions from the lower to the higher centers in the central nervous system* and an increasing dominance of the higher centers in the control of activity. This process of "encephalization" was first systematically studied for motor function (Marquis 1935). The paralysis following removal of the motor cortex is progressively more complete and more permanent the higher one goes up the phyletic scale. A similar process of encephalization is found for the senses (Marquis summarized the data for vision).

In the lower vertebrates such as fish and amphibia, the chief part of the nervous system involved in vision is the optic tectum (the analogue of which in the mammalian brain is the superior colliculus). Removal of the cortex produces no impairment of vision. In reptiles and birds there is the beginning of a cortical visual system, but the optic tectum remains the chief area of the brain responsible for vision. Removal of the cortex in reptiles and birds results in almost no visual defect.

In rodents the cortex is relatively much larger and important for the control of behavior. Complete destruction of the cortex in rabbits produces marked impairment of vision. However, the decorticate rabbit can still discriminate different levels of brightness, avoid obstacles, and recognize its food dish by sight. In dogs, removal of the cortex abolishes all vision, except that of brightness discrimination. In the primates, even brightness discrimination is impaired.

---

* The functional shift involves both the fact that the cortex takes over jobs which are handled subcortically in lower animals and the fact that the higher centers integrate and coordinate activity of the lower areas.

Conclusion

The size, form, and importance of the nervous system change markedly as we ascend the phyletic scale. In the present state of knowledge, it is impossible to detail all the important trends, but it *is* essential for the comparative psychologist to be aware that many of the behavioral trends he notes may be directly related to physiological variations in different species. For example, in Chapter 9 we will note the greater influence of learning, as compared to hormonal factors, on sexual behavior in higher animals. This of course is a direct result of the increased size and dominance of the central nervous system in higher animals and the consequent increasing role of the cerebral cortex in the determination of behavior.

References

Jerison, H. J. 1970. Brain evolution. *Science* 170:1,224-25.

Marquis, D. G. 1935. Phylogenetic interpretation of the functions of the visual cortex. *Archives of Neurology and Psychiatry* 33: 807-12.

Rensch, B. 1956. Increase of learning capability with increase of brain size. *American Naturalist* 90: 81-95.

Tavolga, W. N. 1969. *Principles of animal behavior.* New York: Harper & Row.

Chapter 6

The Senses

In studies of the senses, as well as perception, psychologists have focused on vision, to the neglect of the other senses. Vision is perhaps man's most important sense, so he is more highly motivated to explore it. Since animals other than man are often used to study man, work on sensation and perception in animals has been concentrated on studying their vision.

A second reason for the attention given to vision is the ease with which vision can be studied. In the study of vision it is easy to present both spatial and temporal arrangements of stimuli. With the other senses, this is not as easy. If an animal is to learn to discriminate between two stimuli, it is easy to present the two visual stimuli in close spatial proximity to one another, to place the motivating reward for the animal close to the stimuli, and therefore to insure that it pays attention to both stimuli. If we wished to study hearing, we would have to use temporally separated stimuli, which would introduce the confounding effect of how well the animal could remember a stimulus occurring earlier.

But first, let us look at the distinction between sensation and perception. In this chapter we will be concerned with the equipment the animal has available for sensing and perceiving. We will also look at anatomical structures and how they differ from species to species. Although the psychologist can use the behavioral responses of the animal to study how the senses work, most of the data reported in this chapter will be based on physiological research. We will be looking at the basic, built-in capacity of the receptors to respond to stimulation—in other words, at sensation.*

In Chapter 7 we will look at perception. Perception may be loosely defined as the study of how the central nervous system processes the raw information provided by the sensory structures and in what ways an animal responds to the processed information. Most studies of perception use behavioral measures. In fact, the two areas of sensation and perception overlap to some extent, and some topics can be studied using either approach. Some processing of the raw information provided by the sensory structures occurs in the sensory structure itself, so the distinction between sensation and perception is at times fuzzy.

The best way to define sensation and perception is to talk about them, so let us begin.

The Visual System

The Structures

Almost all animals respond to light. The most primitive form of light sensitivity is that of diffusion and is based on the effect of light on the protoplasmic content of the cell. This kind of sensitivity may depend on reaction to the heat that

---

* It is not my aim here to examine the sensory structures of different animals in detail, but rather to focus on phyletic differences. For a description of the specific sensory structures of particular animals, the student is referred to general textbooks such as Marler and Hamilton (1966), where references to primary source materials can be found.

reaches the cell along with light. Sensitivity to diffuse light is found in the most primitive animals, such as amoeba (a Protozoan), as well as in some more highly developed creatures, for instance, some annelid worms.

Animals with sensitivity to diffuse light may or may not also have specialized light receptors. The Protozoan, *Euglena viridis,* has a pigment spot and a nearby photoreceptor, while annelid worms have specialized photoreceptors.

Most animals have special regions where photoreceptors are concentrated. These regions often occur in small pits, as in the limpet (a small Mollusc). Some species have developed structures that cover the photoreceptors. In the ocelli of insects, the photoreceptors are covered by corneagenous cells, which in some insects have developed into corneal lenses.* Some examples of primitive eyes are shown in Figure 6.1.

The pit eye is a step up in the development of the vertebrate eye from the single receptor of simple animals. The vertebrate eye possesses a layer of photoreceptors located behind a crystalline lens and cornea, which focus light stimuli onto the retina. Gregory (1966) speculates that the recessing of the photoreceptors was selected in the course of evolution because to do so provided protection for the photoreceptors from glare and distracting, peripheral, visual stimuli. Covering the pits with membranes protected the pits from foreign matter; thickening the membranes to produce a lens facilitated the discrimination of details in the visual stimuli. The lens also served to increase the intensity of the visual stimulation of the retina.

The vertebrate eye is not the only way to improve the sensory ability of simple eyes. Two other adaptations have been found. The major, alternative adaptation is the compound eye of insects. The compound eye does not consist of many photoreceptors situated behind a single lens; instead, each

---

* A pit itself also operates to increase visual acuity by eliminating confusing light rays, as a pin-hole camera does. Humans have sometimes used deep pits in the ground in order to see the stars during the day.

FIGURE 6.1

Some examples of primitive eyes, each consisting of the same basic plan of a lens forming an image on a mosaic of light-sensitive photoreceptors. From Walls, 1942.

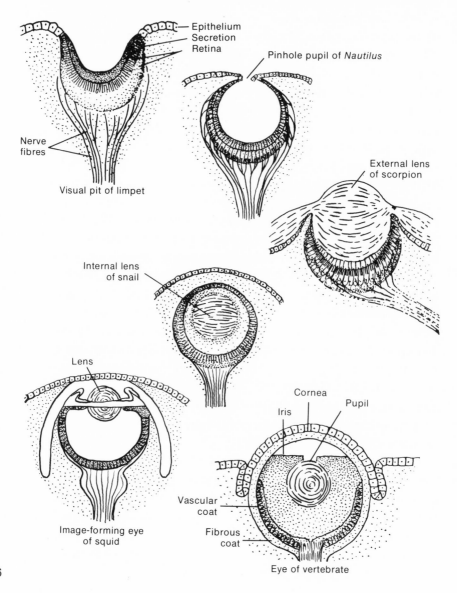

group of photoreceptors have their own lens. The compound eye is made up of many separate ommatidia (simple eyes), each of which has a lens system through which light passes to strike a group of about half a dozen photoreceptors. The number of ommatidia in the insect eye varies from 9 in the eye of the ant *Solenopsis* to 28,000 in the dragonfly eye.

The second adaptation for improving the sensing ability of the eye is comparable to the television camera. In this variation, rather than increasing the number of receptors, it is possible to make one receptor scan the external visual stimulus. Only one animal has been found in which this mechanism is used, the female member of *Copilia quadrata*, a small crustacean (phylum Arthropoda). The photoreceptor system in *Copilia* resembles a single ommatidium (see Fig. 6.2). The two synchronized receptor systems (one on each side of the animal) scan horizontally at a rate varying from one scan every five seconds to one every half second.

The diversity of mechanisms for visual sensing is illustrated by the different ways animals have of accommodating the eye in order to perceive objects at varying distances (Walk 1965). In some animals (for example, most rodents) there is no mechanism for accommodation; in others (for example, snakes) the lens moves to and fro; in man the shape of the lens is distorted; in the ungulates the retina is sloped so that the upper part is permanently accommodated for near objects and the lower part for far objects. In some animals, such as man, both eyes adjust for the distance of the objects, in others (for example, predatory spiders) only one eye adjusts, and in others (for example, flies) only one part of the eye adjusts.

Generally, the higher the animal is on the phyletic scale, the more developed is the structure of its eye. There are many exceptions to this, however, including the compound eye of the Arthropods and the lens eye of some Cephalopods (such as the octopus). Perhaps a better way of phrasing the relationship is to note that the more developed the central nervous system, the more elaborated is the structure of the eye.

FIGURE 6.2
The eye of the female member of *Copilia quadrata.* From Gregory, 1966, p. 30.

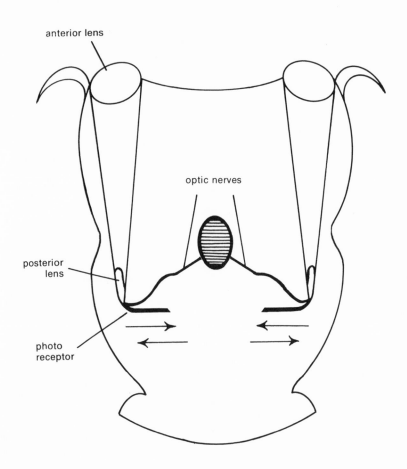

Other structures in the central nervous system are sensitive to light. The pineal gland, which is light sensitive, is important to the response of birds to light. Another light-sensitive structure is the hypothalamus, but it is exposed to light only in experimental situations.

The Sensitivity of Eyes

The eyes of different animals differ greatly in the range of light stimuli to which they are sensitive. The range depends on the particular visual pigments present in the photoreceptors. Animals differ in the number of pigments present. For example, many insects appear to have only one utilizable pigment at night in low illumination. The cockroach appears to have two functioning pigments, which are used in bright light, and the bee has three pigments (Mazokhin-Porshnyakov 1969).

In addition to the number of pigments present, animals differ in the range of sensitivity of these visual pigments (Morgan and Steller 1950). The guinea pig, for example, has three peaks of sensitivity—at wavelengths of 460 mμ (blue), 530 mμ (green), and 600 mμ (red). The rat, on the other hand, has only two peaks of sensitivity, at 500 mμ and 600 mμ. (The peaks indicate the primary colors the animals can react to. They may be red-blind, green-blind, etc.) Fish eyes are sensitive to ultraviolet light, a sensitivity that is most marked in the teleost fishes (class Osteichthyes).

A third difference among animals is in their sensitivity to polarized light (Lester 1970). Many insects (including bees), the octopus, birds, and perhaps man appear to be able to discern polarized light. The evidence is clear concerning insects and the octopus. In man, the evidence that some people can discriminate polarized light comes from the datum that some can see a cross-shaped figure high in a sunlit sky ("Haidinger's brushes"). This is thought to be the result of polarization of sunlight (Lester 1970).

The Auditory System

In order to hear, an animal must have receptors that will respond to vibrations in an elastic medium. There is little evidence that this capacity appears in phyla lower than the Arthropoda. In these lower phyla, however, receptors sensitive to mechanical deformation (touch) can mediate a small amount of sensitivity to vibrations.

Insects have two hearing mechanisms. The first consists of hairs with receptor cells at the base of each. These hairs are extremely sensitive to air currents. Pumphrey (1940) was able to show that they can pick up the Brownian motion of molecules in the air. The frequency range of these structures ranges from 32 to 1,000 Hertz.*

Much less common among insects is a tympanic structure, which may be located on the abdomen (the grasshopper) or the legs (the cricket). The tympanic membrane encloses a pocket of air and receptor cells that are sensitive to movements of the tympanic membrane. The insect responds to the low frequencies superimposed on the very high carrier frequencies detected by this structure. The upper frequency detectable by grasshoppers has been found to be as high as 90,000 Hertz. (In humans the upper limit for perception is 20,000 Hertz.)

Hearing is well developed in the vertebrates, but even here, there are tremendous modifications from fish to mammals. In fish there are again two organs for hearing. The first is a modification of a touch mechanism, the lateral line. Fish have receptors throughout the surface of the body with concentrations along a line on each side. The sensitivity of these receptors is high, but the range of frequencies detected is small and does not extend beyond 300 Hertz. The second organ is a primitive cochlea, the lagena, which is sensitive up to about 6,000 Hertz. As one moves from the fish, through amphibians and reptiles to birds, the lagena becomes more

* A Hertz is one cycle per second.

elaborate until in mammals it is well developed (see Fig. 6.3). The range of frequencies to which the cochlea can respond varies from animal to animal, without systematic trends. The upper limit in the guinea pig is about 40,000 Hertz and in the bat greater than 98,000 Hertz. There are virtually no comparative studies of sensitivity.

Some mammals have developed the ability to use echolocation for guidance in an environment. This is most pronounced in bats and dolphins.* These animals emit high-frequency sounds which are reflected off objects; the echoes are picked up and used to locate the objects and also to tell the animal something about the nature of the objects (for example, the difference between a leaf floating on the surface of a stream and a fish just below the surface).

FIGURE 6.3

The cochlea of vertebrates, (a) unrolled, (b) in cross section, and (c) enlarged (b). From Marler and Hamilton, 1966, p. 413.

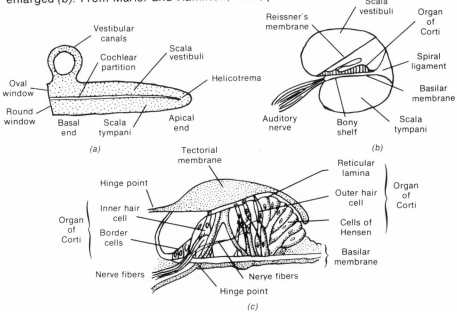

_____

* The ability to use echolocation is also found in other animals—rats and man, for example (Riley and Rosenzweig 1957)—but only in bats and dolphins is it used extensively.

The Chemical Senses

The ability to detect and respond to chemical stimulation is found in nearly all species. The amoeba can approach an object and ingest it on the basis of chemoreception (with occasional, additional cues from tactile sources). Indeed, since almost every animal has to locate food, it makes sense that chemoreceptors should be present in most animals.

Of course, structures for chemoreception become increasingly specialized with progress up the phyletic scale. In very simple animals such as Protozoa, there are no specialized receptors, but such structures are present in the Coelenterates and the Echinodermata. They are increasingly complex in higher animals.

Animals from the Protozoa on up make use of each other's sensitivity to chemical stimulation by means of specialized substances called *pheromones*. In many species, especially among the insects, pheromones are essential for intraspecific (occurring within a species) communication. Ants use a pheromone as an alarm signal which attracts the attention of other members of the colony. When the alarm pheromone is at a low intensity, other ants approach the excited one; when the intensity is high, they attack or flee.

Sex pheromones can act over long distances (2,000 meters or more in the case of some moths) to attract potential mates. In mammals pheromones may have some bizarre side effects. When a group of female mice are caged near a male they can smell, they soon fall into the same estrous cycle. A female mouse in the early stages of pregnancy aborts and returns to estrus when she smells a strange male.

In humans a curious use of sex pheromones is determined by culture. Females carefully wash away the pheromones contained in perspiration and vaginal secretions, but they replace them with perfumes which consist basically of sex pheromones of subhuman species.

Phyletic Trends

I stated at the beginning of this chapter that my aim was not to review the specific details of receptor systems found in different animals, but to look for phyletic trends. One clear trend is for receptor systems to become increasingly more complex the higher the animal is in the phyletic scale. This is especially true for hearing and chemoreception. In vision the trend is less clear, for there occasionally appear in animals complex visual structures that are relatively low in the phyletic scale. For example, cephalopods and insects appear to have highly developed and sensitive eyes.

The second trend is the development of specialized receptors. The amoeba responds to light, chemicals, and tactile stimulation without having specific receptors for them. The stimulation acts directly on the cell constituents. In an animal such as the hydra (a Coelenterate), there are receptor cells, but they do not appear to be specific receptors. The hydra's receptors appear to be equally sensitive to chemical, mechanical, and thermal stimuli.

Two points are important here. First, among animals existing today, specialized receptors appear in very simple organisms; we noted above that *Euglena* (a Protozoan) has a specialized photoreceptor; second, many receptor systems can respond to several kinds of stimulation. For example, if you close your eyes and press on the eyeball through the lid, you will "see" a myriad of colors—visual sensations produced by mechanical stimulation. Receptors can be maximally sensitive to stimulation of one kind, and specialized receptors appear early in the phyletic scale.

The third trend, noted by Maier and Schneirla (1964), is a move from proximal to distal *receptors* as an animal's receptors become more specialized and sensitive. If a receptor is not very sensitive, the intensity of a stimulus has to be quite high for the receptors to react to it. As the receptor system becomes more and more sensitive, it can detect weaker and weaker stimuli and so respond to stimulation emanating from more distant sources. The male silkworm moth (*Bombyx mori*) can detect the odor of a female even if he is several kilometers downwind of her.

It can be argued that there is also a shift from proximal to distal *receptor systems* as one moves up the phyletic scale. Touch and chemoreception become relatively less important, compared to vision and audition. For example, vision is the major sensory modality for some fish and in nearly all birds. The example of the male silkworm moth mentioned in the preceding paragraph indicates that chemoreception is capable of distal reception, but the trend may be valid in general. It would be difficult, however, to provide an *operational* definition of a distal receptor system.

In any case, there are too few data available to test whether there is a phyletic trend. For example, if we used the criterion of the distance at which an organism can detect a stimulus, there are no accurate data from standardized tests to decide between the relative abilities of different animals. The male silkworm moth or the salmon might well possess greater chemoreceptive sensitivity than man and other mammals, but this greater sensitivity might be present only for specific chemical stimuli. Overall, certain mammals might possess greater sensitivity. As usual, it is easier to speculate on phyletic trends than to provide valid and reliable data.

The fourth trend, also noted by Maier and Schneirla, is that there is a greater degree of sensory integration in the higher mammals. In the simplest animals, stimuli in different modalities are cumulative. In the amoeba, for example, weak mechanical stimuli alone or weak light stimuli alone do not produce a reaction, whereas the two stimuli presented closely together can produce a response. In the Molluscs, several kinds of sensory integration can be found, among them: (1)

Different phases of a complex reaction may be governed by stimuli to different sensory modalities. The flight reaction of the scallop *Pecten* to an approaching starfish is governed first by visual stimuli, which cause the scallop to extend its tentacles and make minor movements. As the starfish comes closer, the chemical stimulation from the starfish causes the scallop to close its valves and swim off. (2) Stimuli in one modality can inhibit responses to stimuli in another modality. For example, a snail cannot eat if its foot is touched at the same time the food is presented to its mouth.

In higher animals the complexity and degree of sensory integration is much greater. Mammals can use cues in several sensory modalities to guide a particular response. In man (and perhaps in other primates), if a task is learned using cues in one sensory modality (for example, vision), the organism can generalize the solution to the task using stimuli presented to a different modality (for example, touch).

The greater degree of sensory integration in the higher animals may be a reflection of the greater development of their central nervous systems. The higher animals are capable of greater flexibility, complexity, and variability in their behavior as a result of the increasingly elaborate central nervous system. The greater ability to integrate information from different sensory modalities may be just one aspect of this.

References

Gregory, R.L. 1966. *Eye and brain*. New York: McGraw-Hill.
Lester, G. 1970. Haidinger's brushes and the perception of polarization. *Acta Psychologica* 34:106-14.
Maier, N.R.F.; and Schneirla, T.C. 1964. *Principles of animal psychology*. New York: Dover.

Marler, P.; and Hamilton, W.J. 1966. *Mechanisms of animal behavior*. New York: Wiley.

Mazokhin-Porshnyakov, G.A. 1969. *Insect vision*. New York: Plenum.

Morgan, C.T.; and Stellar, E. 1950. *Physiological psychology*. New York: McGraw-Hill.

Pumphrey, R.J. 1940. Hearing in insects. *Biological Reviews* 15:107-32.

Riley, D.A.; and Rosenzweig, M.R. 1957. Echolocation in rats. *Journal of Comparative and Physiological Psychology* 50: 323-28.

Walk, R.D. 1965. The study of visual depth and distance perception in animals. In *Advances in the study of behavior*, vol. 1, ed. D.S. Lehrman, R.A. Hinde, and E. Shaw, pp. 99-154. New York: Academic.

Walls, G.L. 1942. The vertebrate eye and its adaptive radiation. *Cranbrook Institute of Science Bulletin: Volume 19*.

III
Behavioral Differences

Chapter 7

Perception

INTEREST IN THE comparative study of perception was at a peak in the 1960s, stimulated by Sutherland's work on form perception in the octopus and Gibson's and Walk's invention of a device for studying depth perception—the visual cliff (Fig. 7.1). In the early 1970s, while research is still being carried out on perception, the focus has shifted from comparative studies to those aimed at the basic mechanisms involved, regardless of the species. (This change is in contrast to the topic of learning—which we will review in a later chapter—where the comparative focus is still very strong.)

The lack of interest in a comparative study of perception may be a result of the fact that most of the animals commonly studied by the psychologist do not differ greatly in perceptual skills. In our discussion of the different areas of perception, similarities will be much more common than differences. Furthermore, the perceptual skills of different animals are clearly a result of their sensory equipment. In general, the better the eye, the better the perceptual skills. (This generality takes away some of the excitement from the comparative study of perception.) There has been little comparative work done on perception in many of the sensory modalities; instead, almost all of it has been on vision.

The Perception of Depth

An old and important question asks whether visual perception is innately determined or whether what one can see is governed by experience. This problem is relevant to many questions about humans—for instance, whether there are racial or national differences in perception and whether complex visual stimulation is important to developing infants. Although related work has been done with lower animals, the abilities of human babies are difficult to test because so much time must pass before they are capable of significant movement.

The Visual Cliff

Walk and Gibson (1961) devised an apparatus that is ideal for studying the perception of depth in land animals. The animal is placed on a platform on either side of which is a glass surface a few inches below the level of the platform. On one side there is a textured surface just below the glass, while on the other side there is a textured surface farther below the glass. The animal could easily step down to the textured surface on the shallow side if the glass were absent but would have to jump or fall quite a way on the deep side. If the illumination around the apparatus is arranged suitably, the animal responds to the visual choice of a shallow and a deep surface. The glass eliminates echoes and air currents as cues to the depth of the surfaces, and prevents the animal from falling and hurting itself. This apparatus, shown in Figure 7.1, is called the *visual cliff*.

A variety of animals have been tested for depth perception on the visual cliff by noting whether they chose the shallow or the deep side. All adult land mammals that have been tested with the visual cliff avoid the deep side and prefer the shallow side (see Table 7.1). The only animal that may have a weaker tendency to choose the shallow side is the albino rat, whose vision is poor. Routtenberg and Glickman (1964a) found that albino rats, as infants, often chose shallow and deep sides of the cliff equally, and, as adults, chose the shallow side in 61 percent of their choices. Hooded rats, on the other hand, chose the shallow side in 88 percent of choices when tested as infants, and in 91 percent of choices when tested as adults.

FIGURE 7.1
Drawing of the visual cliff. After Walk and Gibson, 1961, p. 7.

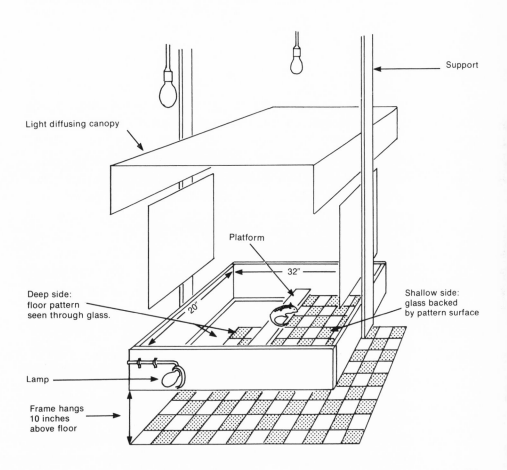

TABLE 7.1
Choices of animals on the visual cliff.

Reptiles

aquatic turtles (e.g., *Pseudomys elegans*)	choose shallow and deep sides equally often (Routtenberg and Glickman, 1964b)
	choose shallow side slightly more than deep side (Walk and Gibson, 1961)
land turtles (e.g., *Terrapena carolina*)	strong tendency to choose shallow side

Birds

chickens	strong tendency to choose shallow side

Mammals

Primates	
monkeys	strong tendency
human infants	strong tendency
Rodentia	
hooded rats	strong tendency
albino rats	weak tendency
gerbils	strong tendency
African spiny mouse	strong tendency
Golden hamster	strong tendency
Carnivora	
domestic dogs	strong tendency
domestic cats	strong tendency
wild cats (lions, tigers, jaguars, snow leopards)	strong tendency
Artiodactyla	
pigs	strong tendency
sheep	strong tendency
goats	strong tendency
Lagomorpha	
rabbits	strong tendency

The chicken also shows a strong tendency to choose the shallow side. Several species of turtle have been tested, and land turtles have shown a strong tendency to choose the shallow side. Turtles that live mainly in the water, however, have been found to show a weak tendency to choose the shallow side by some experimenters (Walk and Gibson 1961) and to show no preference by others (Routtenberg and Glickman 1964b). The aquatic turtle is less likely to encounter situations where it must avoid stepping into a void, so it is logical that the animal has not developed a visual cliff avoidance response to the same extent as have land-based animals.

There does not appear to be any phyletic sequence in the appearance of the visual cliff response. Mammals that live on land show the response, as do birds and land-based reptiles. Small animals such as insects cannot be tested on the visual cliff, for they can walk down the side of the central platform and so are not faced with a visual "cliff." Even with rodents, the platform must be raised sufficiently above the glass so that they are forced to use visual cues rather than information from their vibrissae.

Although the mechanism of the visual cliff response is not relevant here, it should be noted that some features of the response show a phyletic sequence. Some animals are born in a sufficiently developed state to show the visual cliff response from birth. Such animals respond as soon as they can be tested—chickens at three hours (Tallarico 1961) and lambs even at one hour (Lemmon and Patterson 1964). Other animals are not able to see or to locomote at birth and so cannot be tested immediately. Monkeys show the visual cliff avoidance response when they are three days old (Rosenblum and Cross 1963), so three days is sufficient for learning and development of such a response to take place. Human infants have been tested when able to crawl, and they too show the response.*

For some animals the importance of experience and learning in responding to the visual cliff is shown by the fact that deprivation of visual experience affects their performance. Such deprivation does not affect the response of the chicken or the rat. However, 27 days of visual deprivation in the kitten

---

* Using a conditioning technique instead of the visual cliff, Bower (1964) has demonstrated depth perception in the human infant aged 70-85 days.

prevents the immediate appearance of the response. The same is true for rabbits (Walk and Gibson 1961).

It may be that the deprivation of light causes more degeneration of retinal and cortical visual mechanisms in some species than in others. Aside from this possibility, it appears that in the higher mammals (cats, monkeys, and humans, for example), experience of some kind may be necessary for the visual cliff response to occur.

There may be several cues operating in the ability of animals to discriminate different depths (motion parallax, the density of the textured surface, accommodation,* and so on), but there does not appear to be any phyletic sequence in the particular cues used.

Binocular Vision

There are many cues to depth. Among the possible monocular cues are feedback from the accommodation process, motion parallax (which results from movement of the head or body, whereupon nearby objects appear to move relatively more than distant objects), and aerial perspective (in which texture, color, and clarity change with distance). In addition, binocular cues are available to those animals that possess binocular vision, through the degree of convergence and the disparity between the images in each eye.

Animals with binocular vision can be found in many phyla (for example, Mollusca, Arthropoda, and Chordata), but not all animals in these phyla have binocular vision. The presence of binocular vision is associated with the need of the animal for accurate depth perception. Predatory animals have a larger binocular field than do prey animals, whereas animals of prey have a larger total field of view than do predators. Predatory animals need accurate knowledge of their prey's position, while animals of prey need warning of movement in any part

* Changes in the thickness of the eye's lens.

of their visual field. There are no apparent differences in depth perception between predators and prey.

The extent of binocular vision in insects is associated with the speed with which an animal moves. Insects that move rapidly (such as butterflies) have a wider binocular field than do insects that move slowly. (Incidentally, the existence of depth perception in insects has been demonstrated by the fact that insects can distinguish between two-dimentional and three-dimensional objects. The male housefly makes more pre-copulatory jumps toward a three-dimensional female model than toward a two-dimensional model [see Mazokhin-Porshnyakov 1969].)

Reactions to Looming Objects

Schiff (1965) presented the visual stimulus of an expanding or a contracting object to different animals and noted their reactions. The stimulus was a silhouette on a screen. (The presentation of real objects approaching or receding from the animal with no intervening screen introduces air currents and thus less controlled conditions.)

Schiff found that fiddler crabs *(Uca pugnax)*, frogs *(Rana pipiens)*, and domestic chicks all retreated from an expanding dark object. There was a much smaller response to a contracting dark object. For example, 78 percent of the chicks responded to expansion, whereas only 5 percent responded to contraction. When Schiff presented the animals with a light object surrounded by darkness and made the light object expand, even fewer animals responded than when he presented a contracting dark object. Schiff also noted reactions such as flinching and flattening in the species tested.

The reactions were not specific to certain shapes but occurred with any expanding dark object. The frogs and crabs, however, appeared to react less strongly to discontinuous surface shapes than to continuous ones.

Schiff also tested kittens (but used too few to obtain reliable results) and humans (he observed galvanic skin responses rather than motor responses). Menzel (1964) has shown that young chimpanzees respond much as did the species in Schiff's study.

Jumping-Stand Studies

A stand from which an animal is forced to jump to some platform has been used with two species. The desert locust (*Schistocerca gregaria*) will jump accurately onto the nearer of two stimuli. Wallace (1959) gave fourth-instar nymphs* a choice between an object at three inches and one at six inches. The nearer object was jumped upon in 92 percent of the trials and the farther one in 8 percent of the trials. The accuracy of the insect was a direct hit in 88 percent of all jumps.

The rat without training will jump 20 centimeters, with a direct hit in 92 percent of all jumps. At 50 centimeters the percentage of direct hits is down to 20 percent. Training the rat to jump varying distances to avoid electric shock reduces its accuracy (Greenhut and Young 1953). This and the fact that, when presented with different distances in a random order a trained rat does not adjust the force of its jump to the distance to be jumped, has led investigators to conclude that the rat's depth perception is poor. Left to itself, without "training," it appears to cope fairly well.

Effects of Disorientation

The effects of disorientation have been studied in two major ways. In amphibia (frogs and newts) Sperry (1951) surgically rotated the eyes in some cases and in others cut the optic nerves and connected them with the opposite eyes. These surgical manipulations disoriented the animals. For example,

---

* An instar is a stage in the development of an insect and a nymph is an insect in a larval stage.

after the eyes had been rotated 180 degrees, the animals jumped forward to get to an object behind them. The amphibians never adjusted to such disorientations.

A second way in which disorientation can be induced is by the use of displacing prisms placed in front of the eyes of the animals. Hess (1956) displaced the visual fields of chicks by the use of prisms 7 degrees to the side, and found that the chicks did not learn to peck accurately. However, the chicks were studied for only a few days; learning may have taken place after a longer period of time. Also, the chicks found food wherever they pecked, so nourishment was not contingent upon accurate pecking. If it had been, learning might have occurred. Cats (Bishop 1959), monkeys (Bossom and Hamilton 1963), and humans (Howard and Templeton 1966) subjected to displaced visual fields by the use of prisms eventually adapt to the displacement.

It appears, therefore, that those animals in which depth perception is immediate, and which are only slightly affected by dark-rearing, cannot adjust to circumstances requiring reorientation, whereas animals in which visual functioning develops over a period of time *can* reorient.

There seem to be few phyletic trends in depth perception. Accurate depth perception is found in many species and in members of at least three phyla (Arthropoda, Mollusca, and Chordata). The only phyletic trend apparent is that in the mammals of the phylum Chordata, some experience is necessary for accurate depth perception to develop fully. Those species that require such experience appear to be able to adjust to displaced visual fields more easily than those that do not require experience.

The Visual Constancies

The phenomenon of visual constancy is essential for survival. *Constancy* is the name of the process by which objects are seen as keeping the same size, color, shape, etc., even though the viewer's movement or other environmental factors alter the image that falls on the retina. A classic example of constancy is the fact that, though a piece of paper in shadow reflects less light to the eye than a piece of coal in brilliant sunlight, the coal is still seen as black and the paper as white.

The only constancy that has been studied in several species is that of size. Size constancy is the phenomenon whereby the size of objects is perceived correctly even when the size of the image of each object in the eye varies. For example, an animal can be trained to respond to the larger of two objects placed at some distance from him. Then the smaller object is moved nearer to the animal so that its image in the eye of the animal is larger than that of the larger (but more distant) object. An animal showing size constancy will respond to the larger object regardless of the conflicting cue from the retinal size of the image. (Obviously a well-designed study would utilize several objects and insure that the animal was responding to the size of objects rather than to particular objects.)

Size constancy has been shown to be operating in species from three phyla, the Mollusca, Arthropoda, and Chordata (Gibson 1970, Shinkman 1962, Walk 1965). In fact, I was unable to find a report of size constancy not being found in a species. The animals studied, all of which have shown size constancy, are:

Mollusca	cephalopods	octopus
Arthropoda	insects	desert locust (*Schistocerca gregaria*)
Chordata	fish	carp (*Carassius vulgaris*) three-spined stickleback
	birds	chick duckling bluejay
	mammals	weanling rat domestic cat Java monkey chimpanzee two-month-old human infant

The other constancies have not been studied extensively in animals, but there are some reports of hue, whiteness, and brightness constancy in fish, hens, monkeys, and man (Woodworth and Schlosberg 1954). The phenomenon of shape constancy will be considered later in this chapter.

The Visual Illusions

The existence of responses in animals similar to the visual illusions found in man is well documented. The Müller-Lyer illusion[1] has been demonstrated in the chick (Winslow 1933) and the ringdove (Warden and Barr 1929). The horizontal-vertical illusion[2] has been demonstrated in the chick (Winslow 1933), the hen (Revesz 1924), and three species of monkey (Dominguez 1954). The Jastrow illusion[3] has been demonstrated in the hen and the illusion of breadth of rectangles[4] in the chick and three species of monkey by these same investigators. Again, no animal responded to a visual illusion in a way different from man.

[1] The Müller-Lyer illusion

[2] The horizontal-vertical illusion

[3] The Jastrow illusion

[4] The breadth-of-rectangles illusion

Pattern Preferences

The preference of different animals for patterns has been studied, but as is often the case, the studies are not really comparable. Using the visual cliff technique, it was found that all species tested preferred to descend to a textured pattern rather than to an untextured one. Rats and rabbits preferred the larger of two patterns, ducks and goats showed no preference, while chicks preferred the smaller pattern (Walk 1965). Rats, monkeys, and human infants also preferred the more complex of two patterns and spent more time looking at the more complex pattern than at the less complex pattern (Lester 1969).

The Perception of Form

Problems

There are a multitude of studies on the perception of shapes by various species of animals, but from a methodological point of view there are many problems with these studies. First, the studies often are not carried out in such a way that comparison among different species is easy or even possible. This is most clearly illustrated when we compare studies of form perception in insects with studies of other species. The problem is always present, namely were the two species equally motivated? Was the task equally relevant, taking into account the different kinds of life that the two species live?

A second problem—which is the perennial one for comparative psychologists—is deciding whether the failure of an animal to show a particular discrimination or generalization of an already mastered discrimination indicates that the animal *cannot* make the discrimination (or generalization) or that it *will not*. One way to decide between these alternatives is to try to train the animal in optimum circumstances, but then we have to decide whether our final success in training the animal is a reliable occurrence or a chance result.

A third problem is that of determining whether the animal is "in the same experiment as the experimenter." A simple example of this would occur if we trained a rat to discriminate between a square on the left door of a discrimination apparatus and a circle on the right door. The animal may learn the discrimination, but it may have learned a *position* response (left-right) rather than a *stimulus* response (circle-square). We can control for this by placing the stimuli on each door an equal number of times during the training. Nowadays, psychologists do not make these simple errors very often (but see the work later in this chapter on color vision in cats), but the general problem remains. When we train an animal to discriminate between a triangle and a circle, can we be sure it is making this discrimination rather than responding to particular parts of the stimulus—for example, ∧ versus ⌒ rather than △ versus ○ ? But let us leave these cautions and discuss the results of the research.

Mechanisms for Form Perception in Insects and Octopuses

Some insects are able to discriminate between forms, even though early experiments sometimes produced contrary evidence (possibly because the stimuli were too large for the animals to discriminate). To show that the bee (*Apis mellifera*) can distinguish between a triangle and a circle, Mazokhin-Porshnyakov (1969) successfully used stimuli made up of first-,

FIGURE 7.2
From Mazokhin-Porshnyakov, 1969. p. 124.

second-, and third-order figures of the same shapes (Fig. 7.2). Bees can also discriminate between a solid, dark circle and a solid, multipointed star and between solid figures and broken figures.

In other members of the Arthropoda, figure and pattern preferences have been examined, but training has not been used to the extent that it has with the bee. The bee prefers broken geometrical figures over unbroken continuous figures. The diurnal butterfly *Vanessa* and the flies *Lucilia, Calliphora,* and *Sarcophaga* are similar to bees in their preferences, whereas the ant *Formica rufa* prefers shapes with minimal amounts of contour (Mazokhin-Porshnyakov 1969).

The housefly *Musca domestica* and the wasp *Odynerus* appear to be able to discriminate between a square and a rectangle and between squares of different sizes, since they show different spontaneous reactions to these shapes.

The larval forms of insects possess only ocelli, as compared to the compound eyes of adult insects, but the ability of larval insects to perceive shape has been demonstrated. The caterpillar *Lymantria monarcha* prefers objects that taper upward to those tapering downward, and tall triangles to short triangles. It does not react differently to rectangles of different heights which have the same width. Similarly, the nymph of the desert locust *Schistocerca gregaria* prefers long triangles to short ones and vertical edges to slanted edges.

The mechanism proposed for form perception in insects is unlike that proposed for other phyla. The insect appears to use the flicker produced by its movement relative to the object. As the larva moves back and forth in front of the object or as the adult insect flies over the object, the object presents a sequence of stimuli to the eye in the form of light flashes. Complex forms will result in more flashes than simple shapes; it is perhaps on the basis of this flicker that the insect discriminates shape. In support of this theory, it has been observed that bees approach moving flowers more readily than stationary ones (Mazokhin-Porshnyakov 1969).

A similar mechanism is assumed to operate in the larvae of insects, even though they possess ocelli rather than compound eyes. The larvae of several insect species (for example, butterflies, mantises, and locusts) oscillate the front part of their bodies when orienting toward stimuli, a behavior that appears to be consistent with the theory.

To make a contrast with the mechanism proposed above for form perception in insects, let us look at a stimulus-processing mechanism proposed by Sutherland (1960) for form perception in the octopus. Sutherland suggests that the octopus has a shape-analyzing mechanism comprised of a two-dimensional array of cells which count the horizontal extent of a shape at each point on the vertical axis and the vertical extent of the shape at each point on the horizontal axis. The counts are then compared for each shape (see Fig. 7.3).

It can be predicted accurately from this model that the octopus will be able to discriminate horizontal lines from vertical lines, but should be unable to discriminate oblique lines. Sutherland also proposes that the horizontal projection of a form is more important than the vertical projection, which would account for the octopus's better performance in discriminating up-down inversions (⊔ versus ⊓) than lateral inversions (⊏ versus ⊐).

FIGURE 7.3

(a) Sutherland's shape-analyzing model, and (b) horizontal and vertical projections of differently oriented rectangles. From Fellows 1968, p. 156.

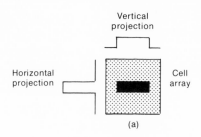

(a)

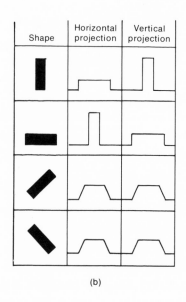

(b)

Work on the receptive fields* of cells in the optic cortex of the octopus has shown that the fields rarely have a diagonal orientation and are more often horizontal than vertical (Young 1960). Wells (1963) has shown that if the ability of the octopus to maintain its eyes in a horizontal position is destroyed surgically, the animal can no longer discriminate between horizontal and vertical lines. Thus physiological studies support Sutherland's theory.

Other stimulus-processing mechanisms are possible, and Sutherland's may not be the only one capable of explaining the known facts. His proposed mechanism, however, does serve to contrast with the flicker mechanism proposed for insects.

The Perception of Form

The perception of form has been studied in one mollusc (the octopus) and several chordates. One problem with reviewing this research is that there is so much of it, yet there is very little organization and systematization in the work. There have been few studies in which standard tests are given to a number of species, so the studies carried out on different animals may not be comparable. Second, no simple categorization of discrimination tasks has been devised. What, for example, are some of the basic dimensions of perceptual recognition? Can they be ordered in terms of difficulty? If we had a series of tasks that tapped each of these basic dimensions, it would be possible to check which animals are capable of which tasks. A third difficulty arises from the fact that the ease of learning a particular discrimination may differ from species to species. Thus some studies present data on the ease with which the discrimination was learned (the slope of the learning curve),

---

* A cell in the central nervous system receives input from many peripheral receptor cells. The receptive field of a cortical cell is the set of receptor cells that transmit information to it.

while others present data on the final performance (the asymptotic level of performance).

Sutherland (1961) has summarized much of the work done on form perception in animals up to 1961. I will try to select from the various tasks he considered those which seem to constitute the basic dimensions of perceptual ability.

1. *Discrimination of orientation*. Two crucial tasks are the discrimination between a horizontal and a vertical line (— versus |) and between two oblique lines (/ versus \ ). All species tested (octopus, fish, rat, cat, dog, and monkey) can learn the former task. Octopuses do not learn the latter discrimination, rats have difficulty, and cats can learn it with little difficulty.

2. *Discrimination between inversions*. A shape can be vertically inverted (⊓ and ⊔) or laterally inverted (⊏ and ⊐). All species tested (octopus, rat, cat, and monkey) learn to discriminate between vertical inversions faster than between lateral inversions. Sutherland noted that no work had been carried out using stimuli with both lateral and vertical inversions (an upside down mirror image).

Actually, the situation here is quite complex. To illustrate this complexity I will mention two facts. Although an octopus can discriminate between ⊔ and ⊓ , it fails to discriminate between ∧ and ∨ . (This can be explained, using the detailed shape-analyzing model proposed by Sutherland and discussed briefly above.) Second, the results from simple discrimination tasks may differ from the results of generalization tasks. For example, our conclusion from a study in which an animal is trained to discriminate between ⊐ and ⊏ may differ from our conclusion from a study in which it is trained to discriminate between R and ∟ and then tested for generalization to Я versus ⌐ .

3. *Discrimination of form*. There do not appear to be any interesting results from this group of studies. Most animals can discriminate between a triangle and a square or a triangle and a circle. Difficulties occur only when the animal pays attention to part of a stimulus rather than to all of it (as in

the case of the rat that pays attention to the base of a figure or the gudgeon that pays attention to the apex).

4. *Generalization.* Animals trained to discriminate between two stimuli usually generalize when the size of the stimulus is altered. That is, if they can discriminate between a large triangle and a large circle, they can also tell the difference between a small triangle and a small circle. On the whole, transfer is better when stimuli are made larger than when they are made smaller. Most animals generalize from solid figures to outline figures. Transfer to dotted outlines is poor. There may be species differences here; fish appear to be worse than birds, for example. Reversing the brightness of figure and ground does not impair the performance of cats and monkeys, but studies on fish, birds, and rats are inconsistent, with some studies showing no impairment and some showing impairment.

5. *Intermodal transfer.* What happens if an animal learns a discrimination using one sensory modality (for example, visual discrimination of shapes) and is then tested using a different modality (for example, tacticle discrimination of the same shapes)? For many animals, of course, limitations of anatomy prevent adequate testing of this ability. Most of the research done has been with primates and has yielded conflicting data. Rothblat and Wilson (1968) have trained monkeys to discriminate between two forms tactually on the basis of size; they found no intermodal transfer when visual discrimination was tested. In other studies Wilson has found evidence of intermodal transfer (Wilson 1965). Davenport and Rogers (1970) did find that orangutans and chimpanzees can observe a visual stimulus and then select by touch alone one of two objects that matches the visual stimulus. Wegener (1965) found no transfer between a visual discrimination, based on the brightness of two objects and an auditory task based on the intensity of the two sounds.*

It is clear from these incomplete data that the tasks used

* Wegener's experiment was poor, in that he made the testing sounds differ in both intensity and frequency rather than only intensity or frequency.

to examine form perception do differ in difficulty. It would be of interest if the tasks could be arranged in a sequence that reflected their differing difficulties. If we could order the tasks in this way, we could then investigate whether they form a Guttman scale (that is, if an animal can learn one task in the sequence, it should be able to master all of the easier tasks in the sequence).

The Relative Importance of Different Cues

One issue that has not yet been systematically studied is, which visual cues are most important for an animal in learning to discriminate between stimuli? An animal may be trained to discriminate between two stimuli that differ in shape, color, brightness, and orientation, but to which cues does it pay the most attention? Some studies that have examined these preferences and the results are:

children	(Hicks and Hunton 1964)	form ⟩ orientation
monkeys	(Hicks and Hunton 1964)	form ⟩ orientation
chimpanzee	(Nissen and Jenkins 1943)	brightness (black versus white) ⟩ size
monkey	(Warren 1954)	color ⟩ form ⟩ size
sheep	(Sutherland 1961)	shape ⟩ color
rat	(Sutherland 1961)	brightness ⟩ shape
rat ⎫ cat ⎭	(see section on the perception of color)	brightness ⟩ color
pigeon	(Jones 1954)	color ⟩ position ⟩ form
fish	(Sutherland 1961)	color ⟩ form
		form ⟩ color

Results vary from species to species. Color is an important cue for the monkey, but relatively unimportant for the sheep. Studies of the relative importance of color and form for fish have produced varying results, depending on the colors used. For some pairs of colors (orange and red), fish respond on the basis of form, whereas for other pairs (dark brown and white or red and blue), they respond on the basis of hue.

It is impossible to draw any comparative conclusions from

these studies, since the techniques used in each study differ. The different results for each species may be the result of variations in techniques rather than true differences between the species.

The Perception Of Movement

The Optokinetic Effect

Mammals exhibit nystagmic movements of the head and eyes in reaction to moving stimuli, and infra-mammalian species show sustained orientation or deviation of the eyes, head, or body. This "optokinetic effect" can be studied systematically by placing animals in the center of a circular drum which rotates around the animal. On the inside of the walls of the drum are vertical stripes which move in a horizontal plane as the drum revolves. This technique has been used to measure the visual acuity of animals by making it possible to note how narrow the moving stripes can be and still elicit the optokinetic effect.

The optokinetic effect has been reported in animals of the phyla Chordata, Arthropoda, and Mollusca (Smith and Bojar 1938). The presence or absence of the response appears to be related to the sensory capacity of the animal. Within vertebrate animals there do not appear to be any systematic differences in acuity; some animals are slightly better than man, while others are slightly worse (Morgan and Stellar 1950).

Discrimination of Movement from Nonmovement

There have been a limited number of studies to determine whether animals can discriminate a moving from a nonmoving stimulus (Kennedy 1936, 1939). Both rats and cats appear able to learn this discrimination. The fish *Betta splendens*

89

(the Siamese fighting fish) was able to learn to discriminate between a revolving black-and-white disk and a stationary gray disk. Both monkeys and bantam chicks were able to discriminate between stimuli revolving at different speeds, and the bantam chick was able to discriminate between stimuli moving in different directions. However, there has not yet been any systematic study of this ability in different species, but presumably, any animal that can chase and capture a moving object can discriminate between a moving object and a stationary one.

Apparent Movement

If two lights, separated by a short enough distance, are illuminated successively, then the spot of light appears to move from one light to the other, provided that the interval between the two flashes is adjusted appropriately. This is called the *phi-phenomenon*.

The phi-phenomenon has been shown in many species which show the optokinetic effect; presumably it is present in all such species. Among insects—animals with compound eyes—shining one light into one ommatidium and another light into a neighboring ommatidium elicits the optokinetic response. The perception of apparent movement has also been demonstrated by illuminating the interior of the rotating drum used to study the optokinetic effect by means of a stroboscopic light (see Smith 1940 for a demonstration of this, using a guinea pig).

Sensory Coding for Movement

Investigators have recently recorded the electrical impulses at various levels of the optic nervous system and noted the electrical response to various stimuli presented to the eye of the organism. Cells have been identified at different levels in the central nervous system of animals; the cells respond only to a stimulus moving in particular directions. For example, Hubel (1963) studied the response of nerves in the optical nervous system of the cat and found cortical cells that respond only to moving stimuli. He identified cortical cells which responded (with electrical activity) when stimuli were moved in particular directions, so that their images on the retina moved across the receptive field of the cortical cell.

Cells that respond to moving stimuli have been identfied in the retina of the frog and the pigeon, in the optic tectum of the frog and the rabbit, in the lateral geniculate nucleus of the thalamus of the rabbit, and in the visual cortex of the cat (Barlow and Hill 1963). In each case the area named is one in which crucial, visual information processing is performed in that species.

It appears, therefore, that the higher the animal in the phyletic scale (at least among the vertebrates), the higher in the central nervous system does the neural processing of information about movement occur.

The Perception of Color

The ability to discriminate between different colors has been demonstrated in many species. This ability is found in most of the higher vertebrates and in the higher invertebrates such as the insects (phylum Arthropoda) and the cephalopods (phylum Mollusca).

Before we review the research, a warning is in order. Reviews of this topic often confuse the ability of the sense organs of an animal to respond to color with the animal's ability to discriminate between colors. (It is easy to show that a cat has the visual apparatus necessary for color vision, but it has proved difficult to obtain behavioral evidence that the cat can discriminate between colors.) We are concerned in this chapter with perception and not with sensation, thus studies of the visual pigments in the retinas of animals or their electroretinograms are not relevant here. Also, when an investigator presents two colored stimuli to an animal, the stimuli will likely differ in brightness. Thus, to insure that the animal is discriminating color rather than brightness, the colors used must be equated for brightness, brightness as perceived by the animal's eye, rather than brightness as perceived by the experimenter. This is not easy and necessitates careful pretesting to measure the brightness of different stimuli as perceived by an animal.

In the phylum Mollusca the cephalopods appear able to discriminate between colors. Squids, cuttlefish, and octopus all show the ability to change skin color to match their surroundings. In addition, some studies have been reported in which cephalopods have been trained to discriminate between different colors. These experiments have not convinced everyone, however. Some authors (for example, Hess 1960) accept the evidence, while others (for example, Thorpe 1963) do not.

Color vision has been demonstrated in many species of insects (phylum Arthorpoda). A common technique is to place appropriate food on a yellow dish, say, and surround the dish with empty dishes colored with varying intensities of orange. The idea is that at least one shade of orange will match the yellow in intensity. Using this technique, it has been shown that both the bee *(Apis mellifera)* and the wasp *(Pseudovespa vulgaris)* appear to have color vision (Mazokhin-Porshnyakov 1969). Insects also spontaneously choose some colors and avoid others, for example, the flies *Lucilia* and *Sarcophaga* prefer yellow.

An animal may not respond to or discriminate between colors in a test we devise, but this could be due to the inadequacy of the test. Thus it is difficult to prove that an animal cannot perceive or discriminate between colors. Mazokhin-Porshnyakov believed that only one insect had been shown to have no color vision, the termite *Hodotermes turkestanicus*. However, other members of the phylum Arthropoda, such as the spiders, appear to be able to discriminate between colors.

In the vertebrates (phylum Chordata), color vision apparently is common; it has been reported in the amphibia, reptilia, birds, fish, and mammals. The problems in demonstrating the ability to discriminate between colors in animals are illustrated by work on the rat (Munn 1950). Attempts in the early part of the century to train rats to discriminate between colors failed. The problem was taken up again in the early 1930s; this time, the results from different investigators conflicted. Munn (1932) could not train rats to discriminate between green and yellow, while Walton (1933) claimed to be able to train rats to discriminate between red and green, but not between green and yellow. Munn (1934) was not able to replicate Walton's results when he introduced adequate controls for differences in the brightness of the colors as perceived by the rat. By the late 1930s, however, most investigators agreed that color vision in the rat had been demonstrated.

The debate over whether the cat can perceive color followed a similar course; only in recent years has color vision been demonstrated. Sechzer and Brown (1964) trained cats to discriminate between colors, and concluded that previous research had failed to demonstrate color perception because the cat was extremely sensitive to brightness differences and its preference for particular brightnesses was difficult to overcome. The cats Sechzer and Brown used also took a great deal of training to make the discrimination—between 1,450 and 1,750 trials.

It is not yet possible to compare the relative abilities of the species which have color vision, for there have been hardly any studies in which several species have been given a similar task.

Phyletic Trends in Perception

The Views of Gibson

Gibson (1970) has argued that perceptual functions can be divided into two kinds, the perception of space (and events in space) and the perception of objects. The perception of space—where one is in space, what events are going on in space, avoidance of obstacles, the food to be approached, and so on—is seen by Gibson as primitive (not only phyletically but also ontogenetically). Learning and experience have little effect on the perception of space and events. The perception involved here is also adaptive in an evolutionary sense. Without these skills an animal would have difficulty surviving.

As examples of this function, Gibson reviewed the studies carried out on different species, and investigated reactions to looming objects, depth perception on the visual cliff, and size constancy. These perceptual functions show few phyletic trends, as we saw above; each is very necessary for the animal if it is to cope adequately with the environment. These behaviors have survival value.

> It is no surprise to the thoughtful biologist that animals other than man exhibit size constancy. How indeed could they locomote or seize things accurately if the apparent sizes of things around them were constantly shrinking or expanding as distance changed with the target's movement or the observer's position? (Gibson 1970, p. 103.)

On the other hand, Gibson noted that there was a phyletic trend in the ability to make fine distinctions between objects. In many animals there is evidence of early identification of some objects. For example, the herring gull chick responds to the spot of red on its parent's beak by pecking and receiving the regurgitated food from the parent. The phenomenon of *imprinting,* whereby the young animal learns during a critical period early in its life which animal to follow and to react to a mother, also requires the young animal to perceive and respond to particular visual cues such as brightness contrast and motion.

Gibson felt that these kinds of responses were rare in lower animals. Lower animals usually respond to gross events and objects. For example, in the work of Schiff, reviewed above, animals reacted to looming objects more or less regardless of the shape and kind of object. Any object was sufficient to produce the avoidance behavior in the animals studied.

Gibson believed that only primates could discriminate well between different forms, such as written symbols. Monkeys can learn to discriminate between pairs of fairly small line drawings, but they are less able at this task than human children four or five years old. Fine discrimination is the most highly developed in man and requires a large amount of learning and education.

Regarding Gibson's thesis, it should be noted that it is far easier to demonstrate experimentally the similarities between species in the perception of space than it is to demonstrate the differences in the perception of objects. Gibson herself cited little data to support the existence of differences in the discrimination of objects by different species. It is possible to document isolated cases in which lower animals surpass even man in the ability to discriminate between objects. For example, Herrnstein and Loveland (1964) trained pigeons to respond to photographs in which human figures were to be found, and noted that on occasion they disagreed with the human decisions, yet were proved correct on closer examination of the pictures. Since visual acuity is excellent in birds, this result is not unexpected.

In general, the higher the animal, the more capable it is of fine discrimination and the more general use it makes of this ability in its environment.

A Physiological Basis for Two Kinds of Perception

Gibson has proposed that the perception of space and the perception of form are two very different processes. Some recent work supports this division of perceptual functions. As Trevarthen (1968) concluded, there seem to be two different visual mechanisms involved in perception. The first is governed by cortical processes and is responsible for "focal" vision, which examines detail in small areas of the visual field. The second is governed by processes occurring lower in the central nervous system (the brain stem appears to be involved here) and is responsible for "ambient" vision, which orients the animal and facilitates locomotion through a visual field. Compared with focal vision, ambient vision has low angular resolution for stationary features, low sensitivity to relative position, orientation, luminance, or hue; but it has high sensitivity to change in any of these attributes.

Trevarthen documented his thesis with data from the effects on the learning of discrimination of breaking the direct neural connections between the two hemispheres of monkeys' cerebral cortex. The "split-brain" monkeys were able without impairment to move, climb, orient, and posture. Discrimination involving both hemispheres was seriously disrupted. Trevarthen argued that ambient vision must therefore be mediated by the more primitive parts of the central nervous system. There are differences in visual functioning of nocturnal and diurnal animals that are related to Trevarthen's description of two visual processes. The nocturnal prosimians, for example, are very good at climbing and catching small animals, but the diurnal higher primates are better at manipulating objects. The latter have better developed color vision and higher acuity, and their eyes are capable of free spontaneous movements.

Gibson interpreted Travarthen's findings and thesis as supporting her concept of two mechanisms for perception that differ in their appearance in the phyletic sequence of animals. But we are not yet able to pinpoint where in the phyletic sequence these perceptual mechanisms begin to develop. If we accept the available data, both mechanisms are present in fish (Ingel 1967), hamsters (Schneider 1967), and monkeys (Trevarthen 1967), so development must have begun prior to the vertebrates.

References

Barlow, H. B.; and Hill, R. M. 1963. Selective sensitivity to direction of movement in ganglion cells of the rabbit retina. *Science* 139:412-14.

Bishop, H.W. 1959. Innateness and learning in the visual perception of direction. Unpublished doctoral dissertation, University of Chicago.

Bossom, J.; and Hamilton, C. R. 1963. Inerocular transfer of prism-altered coordination in split-brain monkeys. *Journal of Comparative and Physiological Psychology* 56:769-74.

Bower, T. G. R. 1964. Discrimination of depth in premotor infants. *Psychonomic Science* 1:368.

Davenport, R. K.; and Rogers, C. M. 1970. Intermodal equivalence of stimuli in apes. *Science* 168:279-80.

Dominguez, K. E. 1954. A study of visual illusions in the monkey. *Journal of Genetic Psychology* 85:105-27.

Fellows, B. J. 1968. *The discrimination process and development.* New York: Pergamon.

Gibson, E. J. 1970. The development of perception as an adaptive process. *American Scientist* 58:98-107.

Greenhut, A.M.; and Young, F.A. 1953. Visual depth perception in the rat. *Journal of Genetic Psychology* 82:155-82.

Herrnstein, R. J.; and Loveland, D. H. 1964. Complex visual concept in the pigeon. *Science* 146:549-51.

Hess, E. H. 1956. Space perception in the chick. *Scientific American* 195(1):71-80.

———. 1960. Sensory processes. In *Principles of comparative psychology,* ed. R. H. Waters, D. A. Rethlingshafer, and W. E. Caldwell, pp. 74-101. New York: McGraw-Hill.

Hicks, L. H.; and Hunton, V. D. 1964. The relative dominance of form and orientation in discrimination learning by monkeys and children. *Psychonomic Science* 1:411-12.

Howard, I. P.; and Templeton, W. B. 1966. *Human spatial orientation.* New York: Wiley.

Hubel, D. 1963. The visual cortex of the brain. *Scientific American* 209(5):54-62.

Ingle, D. 1967. Two visual mechanisms underlying the behavior of fish. *Psychologische Forschung* 31:44-51.

Jones, L. V. 1954. Distinctiveness of color, form, and position cues for pigeons. *Journal of Comparative and Physiological Psychology* 47:253-57.

Kennedy, J. L. 1936. The nature and physiological basis of visual movement discrimination in animals. *Psychological Review* 43:494-521.

———— 1939. The effects of complete and partial occipital lobectomy upon thresholds of visual real movement discrimination in the cat. *Journal of Genetic Psychology* 54:119-49.

Lemmon, W. B.; and Patterson, G. H. 1964. Depth perception in sheep. *Science* 145:835-37.

Lester, D., ed. 1969. *Explorations in exploration*. New York: Van Nostrand Reinhold.

Mazokhin-Porshnyakov, G. A. 1969. *Insect vision*. New York: Plenum.

Menzel, E. W. 1964. Responsiveness to object-movement in young chimpanzees. *Behavior* 25:147-60.

Morgan, C. T.; and Stellar, E. 1950. *Physiological psychology*. New York: McGraw-Hill.

Munn, N. L. 1932. An investigation of color vision in the hooded rat. *Journal of Genetic Psychology* 40:351-62.

————. 1934. Further evidence concerning color blindness in rats. *Journal of Genetic Psychology* 45:285-302.

————. 1950. *Handbook of psychological research on the rat*. Boston: Houghton Mifflin.

Nissen, H.W.; and Jenkins, W.O. 1943. Reduction and rivalry of cues in the discrimination behavior of chimpanzees. *Journal of Comparative Psychology* 35:85-95.

Revesz, G. 1924. Experiments on animal space perception. *British Journal of Psychology* 14:387-414.

Rosenblum, L. A.; and Cross, H. A. 1963. Performance of neonatal monkeys on the visual cliff situation. *American Journal of Psychology* 76:318-20.

Rothblat, L.A.; and Wilson, W.A. 1968. Intradimensional and extradimensional shifts in the monkey within and across sensory modalities. *Journal of Comparative and Physiological Psychology* 66:549-53.

Routtenberg, A.; and Glickman, S. E. 1964a. Visual cliff behavior in albino and hooded rats. *Journal of Comparative and Physiological Psychology* 58:140-42.

————. 1964b. Visual cliff behavior in undomesticated rodents, land and aquatic turtles, and cats (Panthera). *Journal of Comparative Physiological Psychology* 58:143-46.

Schiff, W. 1965. Perception of impending collision. *Psychological Monographs* 79:#11.

Schneider, G. E. 1967. Contrasting visual functions of tectum and cortex in the golden hamster. *Psychologische Forschung* 31:52-62.

Sechzer, J. A.; and Brown, J. L. 1964. Color discrimination in the cat. *Science* 144:427-29.

Shinkman, P. G. 1962. Visual depth discrimination in animals. *Psychological Bulletin* 59:489-501.

Smith, K. U. 1940. The neural centers concerned in the mediation of apparent movement vision. *Journal of Experimental Psychology* 26:443-66.

Smith, K. U.; and Bojar, S. 1938. The nature of optokinetic reactions in mammals and their significance in the experimental analysis of the neural mechanisms of visual functions. *Psychological Bulletin* 35:193-219.

Sperry, R.W. 1951. Mechanisms of neural maturation. In *Handbook of experimental psychology,* ed. S. S. Stevens, pp. 236-80. New York: Wiley.

Sutherland, N. S. 1960. Theories of shape discrimination in octopus. *Nature* 186:840-44.

————. 1961. *The methods and findings of experiments on the visual discrimination of shape by animals.* Cambridge, Eng.: Heffer.

Tallarico, R.B. 1961. Studies of visual depth perception. *Perceptual and Motor Skills* 12:259-62.

Thorpe, W. H. 1963. *Learning and instinct in animals.* London: Methuen.

Trevarthen, C. B. 1968. The mechanisms of vision in primates. *Psychologische Forschung* 31:299-337.

Walk, R. D. 1965. The study of visual depth and distance perception in animals. In *Advances in the study of behavior,* vol. 1, ed. D. S. Lehrman, R. A. Hinde, and E. Shaw, pp. 99-154. New York: Academic.

Walk, R. D.; and Gibson, E. J. 1961. A comparative and analytical study of visual depth perception. *Psychological Monographs* 75:#15.

Wallace, G.K. 1959. Visual scanning in the desert locust *Schistocerca gregaria* Forskal. *Journal of Experimental Biology* 36:512-25.

Walton, W.E. 1933. Color vision and color preference in the albino rat. *Journal of Comparative Psychology* 15:373-94.

Warden, C. J.; and Barr, J. 1929. The Müller-Lyer illusion in the ring dove *Turtur risorius. Journal of Comparative Psychology* 9:275-92.

Warren, J. M. 1954. Perceptual dominance in discrimination learning by monkeys. *Journal of Comparative and Physiological Psychology* 47:290-92.

Wegener, J. 1965. Cross-modal transfer in monkeys. *Journal of Comparative and Physiological Psychology* 59:450-52.

Wells, M. J. 1963. The orientation of octopus. *Ergebnisse der Biologie* 26:40-54.

Wilson, W. A. 1965. Intersensory transfer in normal and brain-operated monkeys. *Neuropsychologia* 3:363-70.

Winslow, C. N. 1933. Visual illusions in the chick. *Archives of Psychology* #153.

Woodworth, R. S.; and Schlosberg, H. 1955. *Experimental Psychology*. London: Methuen.

Young, J. Z. 1960. Regularities in the retina and optic lobes in relation to form discrimination. *Nature* 186:836-39.

Chapter 8

Learning

THE ABILITY of different animals to learn—
that is, to modify their behavior as a result of experience—
provides perhaps the most successful criterion with which to
order the different animal species. In this chapter we will review some of the research pertinent to this issue.

Habituation and Sensitization

One simple form of learning that has been documented
in almost all animal phyla is *habituation*. In habituation a
stimulus is presented to the animal, which makes a response.
A snail's shell is tapped and the snail withdraws. After repetition of the stimulus, the response no longer occurs. By definition, habituation should not be due to sensory adaptation of
the receptors of the animal. The stimulus is indeed received,
but the influence of the central nervous system decrees that
it will not be responded to.

To illustrate the widespread occurrence of habituation, an example of behavior in protozoa may be mentioned. Daňisch (1921) administered mechanical shocks to *Vorticella nebulifera* and noted that the greater the energy of the mechanical shock, the longer it took the animal to habituate its response to the shock. A shock of 500 ergs required nine trials before habituation occurred; a shock of 2,000 ergs required 420 trials. (This study ruled out fatigue as the mechanism underlying the behavior.) Although some authorities argue against this behavior being conceptualized as habituation, it is behavior which, if found in higher animals, would be seen as habituation.

In *sensitization* the opposite phenomenon occurs. Now repetition of stimulation leads to an increased response; again, this has been found in species from all parts of the phyletic scale. Riesen (1960) suggested that the strength of stimulation is the major factor determining whether habituation or sensitization will occur.

Classical Conditioning

If a stimulus regularly produces a particular response in an animal, and if that stimulus is paired with a hitherto neutral stimulus, the neutral stimulus will eventually, after many pairings, produce a copy of the original response. This process is known as classical conditioning. Classical conditioning has been observed in many phyla: Annelida, Echinodermata, Mollusca, Arthropoda, and Chordata. The lowest animal in which classical conditioning has been unequivocally demonstrated is the flatworm *Planaria* (phylum Platyhelminthes). The evidence for classical conditioning in Protozoa is meager and frequently negative (Denny and Ratner 1970).* Razran reported in 1933 that he could find no differences between species in the speed of conditioning or the rate of extinction.

---

* Armus (1970) has claimed that he has demonstrated classical conditioning in a plant!

Instrumental Conditioning

In instrumental conditioning, particular responses of animals are made more likely to occur in given stimulus situations by virtue of reinforcement given to the animal after it has made the particular response.

In the lowest phylum, the Protozoa, Thorpe (1956) has opined that an a priori case has been made for the existence of instrumental conditioning (or associative learning, to use Thorpe's categories), but that critical proof has not yet been provided. For example, Day and Bentley (1911) placed paramecia in small capillary tubes in which ordinary movement was restricted. They timed the speed of the animals in turning around in the tubes and found that the time it took to turn around, as well as the number of unsuccessful attempts, decreased with practice. Various mechanical hypotheses proposed to account for this behavior are either unlikely or unproved. (In fact, the mechanism involved in the behavior is relatively unimportant, compared to the question of the phenomenon's existence. That the mechanism may be different in different species is not relevant.)

Similarly, in the Coelenterates and the Echinoderms, the phenomenon of associative learning is not well established (Thorpe 1956). There are some data suggesting that the behavior may be found in these phyla. Fleure and Walton (1907) fed filter paper to the tentacles of *Tealia* and *Actinia* (members of the phylum Coelenterata); eventually the trained tentacles refused to accept filter paper as food. When the remaining tentacles were tested, it was found that they learned to refuse filter paper much sooner than did the first set of tentacles. *Tealia* exhibited better learning ability than did *Actinia* at this task. Jennings (1907) explored associative learning in the Echinoderms by noting how their righting response, when placed upside down, changed with practice, and concluded that associative learning did take place.

Associative learning is well established in phyletical higher animals: Annelida, Arthropoda, Mollusca, and Chordata.

103

Investigators disagree as to whether species differ systematically in instrumental learning. Warren (1965) argued that there were no meaningful phyletic differences since the variation within species was too large to make between-species comparison useful. (He felt similarly about classical conditioning.) On the other hand, Voronin (1962) argued that there were differences. In studies of vertebrates he argued that species did not differ in their speed of learning, except when inhibitory processes were involved, as in extinction and differentiation and in reversal learning, where the phyletically higher vertebrates learned faster.* Voronin drew an important distinction when he discussed trace conditioning (a classical conditioning behavior) between the first appearance of the learned response and the stabilization of the response. He noted that, for trace conditioning, the first appearance of learning did not vary between species, whereas learning became stabilized sooner in the phyletically higher species.

In his survey of nonprimate learning, Warren (1965) identified many tasks that discriminated between species:

1. Ambiguous conditioned stimuli. That is, the animal must respond to light plus sound, for example, but not to light or sound alone. Baboons can learn this easily; rabbits with difficulty, and fish not at all.

2. Extinction and reconditioning. Among the vertebrates, the phyletically higher species perform faster at this task.

3. Spatial discrimination learning (for example, learning to discriminate two positions). No systematic differences among species.

4. Nonspatial discrimination learning (for example, learning to discriminate two sounds). No systematic differences among species.

5. Intermediate size problem. In this task the middle-sized

---

* Voronin speaks in his article of conditioned reflexes, but he appears to be referring to instrumental conditioning. His paradigm is "bell—dog presses pedal—dog receives food," a Skinnerian situation.

stimulus is the correct one. Rats and cats perform worse at the task than do chimpanzees.

6. Probability learning (dealing with a situation in which one choice is rewarded, say, 70 percent of the time, and the other is rewarded 30 percent of the time). Here there are systematic differences, which will be discussed in detail below.

7. Learning sets (learning to apply an old rule, such as "odd one out," to new problems). Again, there are systematic differences, which we will discuss below.

8. Double alternation problem (learning to make two left turns, then two right, then two left, etc.). Warren noted that it used to be thought that there were species differences, but better methodology has cast doubt on this. Warren felt that there were no species differences.

9. Delayed responding (learning to remember the position of stimuli and to make the right choice after they have been removed). Warren felt the same about this as about the double alternation problem.

10. Multiple sign learning. Performance varies greatly with species in tasks where the animal must learn that a particular stimulus is associated with reward only when it is paired with another specific stimulus. For example, only cats and primates can master the following conditional discrimination, in which the animal must learn all four discriminations, with the tasks being presented in random order during training:

Task I: small black circle + small white circle −
Task II: large white circle + large black circle −
Task III: small white circle + large white circle −
Task IV: large black circle + small black circle −

The animal must learn that the reward value of a stimulus depends on the pair in which it is presented at a particular time.

In oddity problem-solving (where the animal must respond

to the odd one of three stimuli), evidence for learning has been obtained in birds, rats, cats, and raccoons, but the animals often fail to reach criteria. Monkeys and chimpanzees can solve these problems. In addition, monkeys can solve complex oddity problems—for example, to choose the odd form when the background is black and the odd color when the background is white (Harlow 1943).

Qualitative Differences in Learning

Bitterman (1965) has reported species differences in two tasks, habit reversal and probability matching. In habit reversal an animal is trained to choose one of two stimuli by being rewarded for a particular response to one of the stimuli, after which the reward is given only if the animal chooses the other stimulus. After the animal has learned this, the reward is switched again, and so on. Bitterman has studied the performance of animals at this task for both visual and spatial discrimination. The data he has obtained are shown below:

| | Habit Reversal | |
	spatial	visual
monkey	I*	I
rat	I	I
pigeon	I	I
turtle	I	NI†
decorticate rat	I	NI
fish (mouthbreeder)	NI	NI
cockroach	NI	NI
earthworm	NI	NI
* improvement	† no improvement	

Two points stand out. First, animal species differ in their ability to do a habit-reversal task. Second, as one ascends the phyletic scale, the new mode of adjustment appears first in a spatial rather than a visual context.

A second task studied by Bitterman involves rewarding

one stimulus, say, in 70 percent of the trials and the other in 30 percent. Which alternative does the animal choose? Some species show random matching; that is, the animal matches the reward probabilities randomly, choosing one stimulus in 70 percent of the trials and the other in 30 percent of the trials in the example above. Some animals show maximization of reward, always choosing that stimulus rewarded in 70 percent of the trials. Bitterman's data are:

Probability Matching		
	spatial	*visual*
monkey	NM*	NM
rat	NM	NM
pigeon	NM	M†
turtle	NM	M
decorticate rat	NM	M
fish (mouthbreeder)	M	M
cockroach	M	M
earthworm	M	M
* no matching		† matching

Again two points stand out. First, species differ in their behavior in this task, and second, the new mode of adjustment appears first in the spatial context and later in the visual context. A third point to note is that it seems that this task might be placed higher in a scale of phyletic difficulty than the task of habit reversal. Fewer species of animals show nonmatching in a visual task than improvement in habit reversal in a visual task.

Bitterman made several other points. Differences between species may be a result of differences in sensory, motor, or motivational factors. It is difficult, if not impossible, to control (or even measure) these factors. Bitterman noted, however, that the differences he reported hold up when the species are tested under different conditions. Furthermore, qualitative differences are likely to be more valid (that is, independent of the testing conditions) than quantitative differences between species.

Bitterman also noted other differences between species. For example, rats and monkeys behave differently in probability matching tasks. Rats tend to choose the alternative rewarded on the previous trial, while monkeys tend to avoid it. This different strategy in the monkey is found in spatial discriminations but not in visual discriminations, again illustrating the differences between spatial and visual tasks. Bitterman noted that further discrimination between species may be possible by differentiating between different strategies of nonmatching in probability learning, such as maximizing, near maximizing, and nonrandom matching of different kinds.

Warren (1965) pointed out that there are differences in the results of these comparisons, depending on whether the task is a reversal learning set using one task, or a learning set using different tasks each time. Warren felt that the latter task achieved a better discrimination between the abilities of mammalian species.

Qualitative or Quantitative Differences?

Gossette (1968) has pursued the study of habit reversal in a variety of species; he noted that there are two main hypotheses about the variation. First, the discontinuity hypothesis advanced by Bitterman asserts that improvement from trial to trial is shown by some species and not shown by others. Gossette argued that recent studies have found that teleost fish improve with practice and that turtles improve with practice in a visual discrimination task. He argued, therefore, that a continuity hypothesis may be more valid. In this approach, species are not divided into those that show improvement and those that do not, but rather are considered in terms of the quantitative differences in the rate of improvement.

If the differences are viewed as quantitative, the control of motivation becomes crucial. In a series of studies, Gossette has endeavored to control for motivational differences in different species and has found reliable species differences that appear to be related to various indices of brain complexity. The number of errors made by different species in an initial spatial habit-reversal problem, and subsequent reversals, is shown below.

mammals	capuchin monkey	54.2
	cacomistle	81.0
	raccoon	157.7
	skunk	193.8
	coati mundi	203.8
	squirrel monkey	208.5
	kinkajou	253.7
birds	Himalayan magpie	161.3
	white king pigeon	194.4
	Guinea fowl	677.8
	white leghorn chicken	619.6
	trumpeter	1332.0

Gossette has developed a *taxonomic distance hypothesis* in which similarity of habit reversal performance is a function of interspecies taxonomic distance. Gossette has also tended toward a phyletic (or rather a phylogenetic) distance hypothesis. He has argued that the magpie (a relatively advanced bird phylogenetically) would perform better than the trumpeter (a relatively primitive bird phylogenetically). What lies behind these differences? The habit reversal task combines inconsistent reinforcement with a maximal opportunity for negative transfer to occur. Gonzales et al. (1967) have argued for a retention-decrement hypothesis in which the species that perform poorly in the task "fail to forget" what is learned in the previous task (that is, there are differences in proactive interference). Gossette has offered a differential extinction hypothesis in which it is not the rate with which an organism learns to respond to a stimulus that is crucial, but rather the rate with which it learns to inhibit responding as a consequence of nonreinforcement.

It should be noted before leaving this topic that Bitterman (1969) has not yet abandoned his position that the differences are qualitative and not quantitative.

Learning as Inhibition

The notion that species differ most in behaviors that require inhibition has come up frequently in this chapter. Animals seem to differ more, for example, in extinction of learning than in learning, which Harlow (1958) has elaborated on.

Harlow noted that there do indeed appear to be large differences in the learning capacities of different phyla. He proposed a rough ordering of species, as follows:

> protozoa
> echinodermata and coelenterata
> flatworms
> annelida
> octopus
> teleost fishes
> subprimate mammals
> primates

Harlow suggested that the differences between these species may not be very great. He argued that a relatively small intellectual gain by man over the anthropoids, for example, could make possible the development of symbolic language and culture. He noted that a fledgling swallow, a few days before it can fly, differs only slightly anatomically and physiologically from the swallow a few days later, when it can fly. Yet in terms of achievement the difference appears to be great. Harlow argued, therefore, for a basic similarity underlying all learning in different species—an inhibition process. Learning consists of inhibiting inappropriate response tendencies.

Paramecia, if placed in a tube from which they escape via the base, do so with increasing speed on successive trials. Harlow argued that the paramecia come to inhibit inappropriate swimming movements. The sea anemone will at first convey nonedible materials to its mouth by means of its tentacles, but after a few repetitions will no longer do so. This inhibition is specific to the tentacles used. Other tentacles will still convey the materials to the mouth, and so on. Harlow takes different animals in different learning situations and shows how the inhibition of inappropriate responses plays a crucial part in their learning of different tasks.

The importance of Harlow's views for us lies in the fact that they emphasize the similarity between the learning of different species. The gulf between the learning capacity of animals may not be as large as some writers believe. For example, "Man is not simply a very clever ape, but a possessor of mental abilities which occur in other animals only in most rudimentary form, if at all." (Dobzhansky 1955, p. 338.) Harlow characterized such views as "specism."

Odds and Ends

There are many other behaviors that might prove interesting when compared throughout species, but little systematic work has been done on these behaviors. Included here might be such dimensions as the number of learned responses that can be concurrently functional in the animal, the duration of learning (that is, the animal's memory), and whether the animal shows evidence of reasoning and insightful behavior.

The studies of reasoning in the rat by Maier and insight into chimpanzees by Köhler are well known and warrant discussion here. Although it seems valid to conclude that the phyletically higher the animal, the better able it is to engage in reasoning and insightful behavior (difficult though these terms are to define), the comparative psychologist's problem is that it is difficult to devise comparable tasks for different species, which would yield the data needed to demonstrate this. For example, Köhler's chimpanzees stacked boxes in order to reach food hung high up without showing typical trial-and-error behavior in devising this response. (It should be noted here that Schiller (1952) observed chimpanzees stack boxes and climb on them in play when no food was around.) How can one devise a comparable task for cats, or rats, let alone for

111

octopuses or for bees? It might be difficult to observe or define insightful behavior in a species whose behavioral repertoire is greatly different from ours. To illustrate this argument, an example can be taken from intelligence testing. It is argued that intelligence tests designed by white middle-class psychologists are not appropriate measures of intelligence in nonwhite populations. There is a cultural bias in the intelligence test. In a similar way, there may be a "species bias" in our tests of the ability of animals to learn.

References

Armus, H. L. 1970. Conditioning of the sensitive plant, *Mimosa Pudica*. In *Comparative Psychology,* by M. R. Denny and S. C. Ratner, pp. 597-600. Homewood, Ill.: Dorsey.

Bitterman, M. E. 1965. Phyletic differences in learning. *American Psychologist* 20:217-27.

———. 1969. Habit-reversal and probability learning. In *Animal discrimination learning,* ed. R. M. Gilbert and N. S. Sutherland, pp. 163-75. New York: Doubleday.

Danisch, F. 1921. Ueber Reizbiologie und Reizempfindlichkeit von *Vorticella nebulifera. Zeitschrift fur allgemein Physiologie* 19:133-88.

Denny, M. R.; and Ratner, S. C. 1970. *Comparative Psychology.* Homewood, Ill.: Dorsey.

Day, L. M.; and Bentley, M. 1911. Note on learning in paramecium. *Journal of Animal Behavior* 1:67-73.

Dobzhansky, T. 1955. *Evolution, genetics, and man.* New York: Wiley.

Fleure, H. J.; and Walton, C. L. 1907. Notes on the habits of some sea anenomes. *Zoologischer Anzeiger* 31:212-20.

Gonzales, R. C.; Behrend, E. R.; and Bitterman, M. E. 1967. Reversal learning and forgetting in birds and fish. *Science* 158:519-21.

Gossette, R. L. 1968. Examination of retention decrement explanation of comparative successive discrimination reversal learning by birds and mammals. *Perceptual and Motor Skills* 27:1,147-52.

Harlow, H. F. 1943. Solution by rhesus monkeys of a problem involving the Weigl principle using the matching-form-sample method. *Journal of Comparative Psychology* 36:217-27.

———. 1958. The evolution of learning. In *Behavior and evolution,* ed. A. Roe and G. G. Simpson, pp. 269-90. New Haven: Yale Univ. Press.

Jennings, H. S. 1907. Behavior of the starfish *Asterias forreri* de Loriol. *University of California Publications in Zoology* 4:53-185.

Razran, G. H. S. 1933. Conditioned responses in animals other than dogs. *Psychological Bulletin* 30: 261-324.

Riesen, A. H. 1960. Learning. In *Principles of comparative psychology,* ed. R. H. Waters, D. A. Rethlingshafer, and W. E. Caldwell, pp. 177-207. New York: McGraw-Hill.

Schiller, P. H. 1952. Innate constituents of complex responses in primates. *Psychological Review* 59:177-91.

Thorpe, W. H. 1956. *Learning and instinct in animals.* Cambridge, Mass.: Harvard Univ. Press.

Voronin, L. G. 1962. Some results of comparative-physiological investigations of higher nervous activity. *Psychological Bulletin* 59:161-95.

Warren, J. M. 1965. Primate learning in comparative perspective. In *Behavior of non-human primates,* vol. 1, ed. A. M. Schrier, H. F. Harlow, and F. Stollnitz, pp. 249-81. New York: Academic.

Chapter 9

Motivated Behavior

An IMPORTANT QUESTION for psychologists in the past concerned the energizing of behavior. What makes an animal make any response or show any activity? This question was formerly asked because the organism was considered as quiescent until acted upon by some stimulus. The analogy often used was that of a billiard ball which remains inactive until struck and then moves only until the energy put into it dissipates.

Today the question is no longer asked, not because the answer is known and accepted but because the question is meaningless within our present intellectual framework. The organism is no longer viewed as a quiescent object. Instead, it is seen as constantly active, with the activity taking various forms. For example, there is always electrical activity in the brain, even in sleep and comatose states. The presence of electrical activity is considered to be a criterion for judging an animal to be alive. Even in sleep, a relatively quiescent state, there can be one of several patterns of electrical activity in the brain. There may be rapid eye movements, motor movements (tossings, twitchings, bladder emptyings, and so on), vocal noises, and activity that is later recalled and labeled as dreaming.

Since the organism is now considered to be energized unless dead, the question of motivation as originally phrased is no longer an issue. There still remain many fundamental questions and issues in motivation, though, and these have relevance for comparative psychology.

The Number and Complexity of Motives

Animals are always engaged in some kind of activity. We may ask the question, "What directs the animal to engage in one kind rather than another?" "What motivates the animal to do this rather than that?" We can also ask whether the choice of behaviors open to an animal shows any trend throughout the species. Do some species show more motives in their behavior than others?

We can define motivated behavior in terms of the end, goal, or purpose of the behavior. Examples of motivated behavior commonly studied by psychologists are hunger (the goal of food), sexual behavior (the goal of coitus or orgasm), exploratory behavior (the goal of sensory stimulation), achievement behavior (the goal of success in some task), and affiliation behavior (the goal of being with another animal).

What we find is that, in general, the higher the animal, the more kinds of motivated behavior we can document. Some animals show a richer variety of behavior and to these we attribute a greater variety of motives. Man is seen as having the most motives, which may reflect a valid fact or merely our greater understanding of man, gained through introspection. Whether a nonhuman observer of human behavior would classify so many motives is an unanswerable question. Maybe we would be judged as the most complexly motivated animals in any case, but since we make the rules and definitions, we must of necessity win the complexity contest.

A distinction is often made between viscerogenic, or biogenic, motives (those with obvious biological bases) and
116   psychogenic motives (learned motives). For motives such as

hunger we can document how nutritional deficiencies antedate and direct the behavior of the organism. Similarly, thirst, elimination, and to some extent sexual behavior have biological determinants that are relatively easy to describe and demonstrate. Biological motives appear to be almost universal. All animals ingest some kind of nutritional objects.* Most have some system for getting rid of waste products, and the majority of species reproduce sexually.

On the other hand, some animals appear to be able to acquire motives in addition to those biology provides. This is a step up in complexity. It seems generally true that the higher the animal, the more motives it can learn or acquire.

As an example of psychogenic, or learned, motivation, we may note that humans frequently (at least in our culture) appear to seek money. A large amount of activity is directed toward acquiring and hoarding it. This motive is a learned motive. The small infant does not have a need for money and requires a good deal of socializing by his parents, teachers, and peers before he manifests such motivation. For some people, money is sought primarily as a means of acquiring other objects, such as food. On the other hand, for some individuals the acquisition of money itself becomes a goal. We say that the seeking of money is an acquired, or learned, motive, a psychogenic motive.

Classifying motives as learned or unlearned is a very difficult task. Some psychologists consider stimulation-seeking to be a learned motive. It can be learned, for instance, on the basis of prior association with primary biological goal objects. An animal might have originally "explored" in order to find food. This behavior could be rewarded by the animal finding food. Thus the animal learned to move about in a way that we, as psychologists, label "exploratory behavior." The animal is exploring, perhaps, because these movements have in the past been associated with food. Novel stimulation (the goal of exploratory behavior or stimulation-seeking)

* Some animals eat in the larval stage, but do not eat when they become adults.

acquires secondary reinforcing properties and eventually may be sought for its own sake. Other psychologists would argue that stimulation-seeking is not learned, but rather is present from birth. For example, Mason and Harlow (1959) showed that monkeys with no prior experience with solid food manipulated and ate food that presented a more complex visual stimulus to a greater extent than food that presented a less complex visual stimulus. The newborn human infant will orient itself to a more complex visual pattern almost as soon as it can be tested after birth (Berlyne 1958).

Despite the difficulty of classifying motives into learned and unlearned, it appears likely that the higher animals have a greater number of motives and that this greater number of motives is primarily due to the appearance of a greater number of learned motives.

Maslow's Hierarchy of Motives

Maslow (1954) classified five kinds of motives: physiological motives, safety motives, belongingness and love motives, esteem motives, and self-actualization motives. Physiological needs include food, water, oxygen, and elimination.* They are *isolable;* that is, they are relatively independent of one another and tend to be *localizable,* that is, associated with certain parts of the body. For example, thirst can be localized to water deficiencies in the cells of the body, dryness in the mouth and throat, and to specific structures in the central nervous system (the hypothalamus). (The behaviors associated with these physiological needs can of course be used as channels for expressing or serving other motives as well. People sometimes eat when they are bored or when they are anxious.)

Safety motives are evident in the preference of children for undisrupted routines and rhythms and their preference for a predictable, orderly world. If an organism is presented

* These correspond to the biogenic motives mentioned above.

with unfamiliar objects or stimuli, the organism may move to a familiar and secure locale. For example, a child placed in a strange room with its mother will cling to its mother.

The motives of belonging and love are manifest in the need for friends, a spouse, and children. There is a need for affectionate relationships with other people, for a place in a group of people. The esteem motives are manifested by our desire for a stable, firm, high evaluation of ourselves, for self-respect and self-esteem, and for the esteem of others. There are two motives at work here: the need for achievement and mastery, which we acknowledge, and a need for reputation and prestige, which others acknowledge.

Finally, there are self-actualization motives. A man must do what he is fitted for; he must realize his full potential and achieve that which he is capable of doing. He must actualize his capacities.

According to Maslow, these five sets of motives form a hierarchy. The lower needs must first be satisfied before the higher needs can be attended to. If we are starving, we are less likely to be concerned with esteem needs. If we lack love and a place in a social group, we may ignore and not even be aware of our self-actualization needs.

There is also an ontogenetic sequence in the hierarchy. At birth, children need only food and safety. Later they need love, and still later self-esteem. As for self-actualization, even Mozart had to wait until he was three before he could begin writing music.

Finally, there is a phyletic sequence in the motives. Physiological motives are almost universal, the safety motives less so. The need for love and to belong begin to appear in the vertebrates and especially the higher mammals. The need for self-actualization may be found only in humans.

The Directing of Behavior

At last it is time to turn to the problem of the direction of behavior. Why does an animal do one thing rather than another? The mechanisms behind the directing of behavior are varied. I could detail the different mechanisms underlying, say, eating behavior in different species, but in this book we are looking for phyletic trends rather than a mere cataloguing of differences. Let us take an example, that of sexual behavior, and see if there are any identifiable phyletic trends.*

Sexual behavior occurs in most species, though not all (see Table 9.1). There are only three major phyla in which sexual behavior does not occur: the sponges, coelenterates, and echinoderms. All of these phyla are predominantly marine animals and are either sessile as adults or sluggish in their movements.

TABLE 9.1
The occurrence of sexual behavior in the animal kingdom.
From Scott 1961, p. 133.

Phylum	No sexual be- havior	Differ- entiated sexual behavior common	Functional Hermaph- roditism common	Asexual as well as sexual repro- duction common
Protozoa (one-celled animals)				x
Porifera (sponges)	x			
Coelenterata (coral and jellyfish)	x			x
Echinodermata (starfish, sea urchins)	x			
Platyhelminthes (flatworms)			x	x
Nemathelminthes (round- worms)		x		
Annelida (segmented worms)			x	
Arthropoda (crustaceans, insects, spiders)		x		
Mollusca (snails, bivalves, squids)		x	x	
Chordata (vertebrates)		x		

* The initial part of this section draws heavily on the writings of Scott (1961).

Sexual reproduction is occasionally found in one-celled animals. In paramecia, reproduction can occur by simple cell division, but under certain conditions two paramecium cells can join their oral surfaces and exchange nuclei, after which they divide into four smaller paramecia.

The development of sexual behavior can take two forms. The first is toward hermaphroditism, in which one animal has both male and female organs. This is found in many worms (flatworms, tapeworms, earthworms) and in molluscs (snails). Only one species of vertebrates is hermaphroditic, the fish *Serranelus subligarius*. In hermaphroditic reproduction two animals usually come together and mutually exchange sperm.

The more general phyletic trend is toward differentiation of sex behavior, with males becoming more active and females more passive. But there are exceptions. For example, the male annelid worm *Bonellia* lives within the body of the female as a parasite. Other species (insects such as ants and bees) can develop into mature animals without fertilization. In the wasp *Nemeritis* there are no males. In many higher animals, sexual behavior is not only more complex and elaborate but has also taken on a secondary function unrelated to reproduction, namely facilitating and stimulating social coherence and coordination. Among the vertebrates (especially some birds and mammals) sexual pairings may last a long time, even for life. Such pairings are an important example of the way in which the social life of vertebrates differs from that of insects. In the latter, sexual behavior plays a minimal role in coordinating the social life of the group.

There are perhaps some trends in the mechanisms involved in sexual reproduction throughout the phyletic scale, although they are far less clear than those discussed above. As an example here, we can consider the means used to insure that coitus leads to fertilization. In some species such as bats and honeybees, the male sperm are stored inside the female's body over long periods of time after coitus, until they are needed for fertilizing ova. In other species, the female's behavior facilitates fertilization. The guinea pig comes into heat (behaves in a sexually receptive way) just eight hours before ovulation, thus insuring that sperm will be available when the egg is released. In cats vaginal stimulation from the penis stimulates the female's pituitary gland, which releases the hormones that cause ovulation. In monkeys, the mechanism operates through repeated coitus during the time when ovulation may occur. The prolonged sexual interaction involved in this latter mechanism plays an important part in the social organization of the primates.

Beach (1947,1969) has examined in detail the mechanisms underlying sexual behavior in animals. He has shown that, in lower animals, coital performance depends heavily on hormones from the reproductive glands, whereas in the animals higher on the phyletic scale (and in particular, monkeys and man), the rigidity of hormonal control is less, so that sexual responsiveness and potency can survive in the absence of sexual secretions. For example, ovariectomy of the female rat prevents her from ever becoming sexually receptive again. When the male rat is castrated, his sex behavior deteriorates more gradually, but in a few months he shows little sex behavior. The effect of these operations is much less severe in dogs. (In most species the hormonal components are more important for the sexual behavior of females than for that of males. In female dogs hormones are necessary, though not sufficient by themselves, for the appearance of sex behavior. Sexual behavior in male dogs can survive to some extent removal of the source of sexual hormones.) There are many reports of sexual behavior in humans remaining unaffected by castration and ovariectomy.

Beach also noted the effect of the development of the central nervous system on sexual behavior. The greater development of the central nervous system leads to a greater involvement of cortical direction in behavior, which in turn means greater variability, flexibility, and an increasing dependence on experience. Beach also noted that the increased role of the cortex in the direction of sex behavior results in increase in the kinds of sensory input that stimulate sexual behavior. In humans, for example, sex behavior can be aroused by stimuli possessing no biological sexual significance (as, for example, in the case of fetishism). Insofar as one can contrast the contributions of inheritance and experience with the determination of behavior in a species, the higher animals, because of the greater role of the cortex in sexual behavior, have their sexual behavior determined to a greater extent by experiential factors than do the lower animals.

The Variability of Behavior

The final issue in motivation is the variability of the animal's behavior. When carrying out an act, the exact sequence of behavior of an animal changes from trial to trial. For example, if a rat runs from a start box to a goal box for a food reward through a complex maze, it will change its path on each trial (Krechevsky 1937).

One of the simplest ways to study the variability of behavior is through the phenomenon of response alternation. If an animal is made to turn left, say, in a maze, when it reaches the next choice point, it may make the same turn (left) as was previously forced or it may make the opposite turn (right). If the animal were to make the opposite turn, then it would be varying (alternating) its response. I reviewed the research on this topic (Lester 1968) and reported that the phenomenon of response alternation was found in insects (including the sowbug *Porcellio scaber,* the meal worm *Tenebrio molitor,* and many other bugs), and in man. For other organisms, the data conflict; some investigators obtained response alternation and others got chance responding by the animals (for example, in paramecia, planaria, earthworms, and rats). In some animals (ants and chickens) response alternation has never been reported. The fruit fly *Drosophila melanogaster* shows response repetition. I was unable to account for the species variation in the manifestation of this phenomenon.

Exploratory behavior involves an animal seeking out novel stimuli or varying his sensory input and so is relevant here.

Exploratory behavior, in which animals investigate the locale in which they find themselves, is found in almost all species that are capable of movement. In order to exist in an environment, an animal needs some information about its environment. However, the particular behaviors that constitute exploration may be more difficult to observe in some species than in others.

Glickman and Sroges (1965) have studied species differences in exploratory behavior. They gave zoo animals objects to investigate. There were large differences in the behavior of different orders of animals. The primates showed the most orienting responses to the objects, followed by the carnivores, rodents, marsupials, ungulates, and primitive mammals, with the reptiles the least responsive. In contacting the objects, the order was similar except that the carnivores were more responsive than the primates. Glickman and Sroges concluded that those orders with more developed neuromuscular systems were more reactive. Within orders, however, no trends appeared. The lower carnivores were less reactive than the higher ones, but higher and lower primates were equally reactive. For example, among the carnivores the *Felidae* and the *Canoidae* were three times as reactive as the *Viverridae*. Among the primates, on the other hand, each of the major groups (the New World monkeys, the Old World monkeys, and the Old World prosimians) contained some families that were very reactive and some that were relatively unreactive.

Glickman and Sroges felt their data supported the view that the more intelligent species were quantitatively more reactive to novel stimuli.

When an animal is presented with a novel stimulus, it pricks up its ears, looks toward the stimulus, and shows a variety of other motor responses. This response to a novel stimulus is called the "orientation reaction" and has been studied intensively in the USSR. It has many components: increase in the sensitivity of sense organs, changes in the skeletal muscles that direct the sense organs, changes in general skeletal musculature, EEG (electroencephalogram) changes, and vegetative changes. Lynn (1966) has reviewed the literature on the orientation reflex and noted several phyletic trends.

It is generally believed that the orientation reaction shows a phyletic trend occurring in its most adequate form in the primates. Some form of orientation reaction, however, is found in many species, especially the vertebrates.

The phyletically higher animals have more pronounced orientation reactions, especially in the somatic components. For example, the reaction in monkeys lasts longer than that in dogs. The reaction of dogs, which is more pronounced, facilitates reception of the stimulus (for example, head movements toward the stimulus, pricking up the ears), as compared to the reactions of carp and pigeons.

The reactions habituate (weaken and disappear), sooner in the phyletically higher animals. Monkeys habituate sooner than dogs and reptiles, while birds show little habituation. The reaction appears sooner after birth in phyletically higher animals. Once an animal has habituated to a novel stimulus, it is easier to disinhibit the orientation reaction in dogs and polecats, for example, than in pigeons and fish. Finally, it has been noted that stimuli which are significant for a species evoke orientation reactions that are very resistant to extinction. Thus a rustling noise elicits a reaction in dogs that habituates easily, whereas in hares the reaction is highly resistant to extinction.

I have investigated the exploratory behavior of different species (Lester 1969) and noted that the kinds of theories proposed to account for exploratory behavior get more complex as one moves up the phyletic scale. To account for response alternation in paramecia, an explanation in terms of centrifugal swing (overshooting the turn in the stem of the T-maze), plus thigmotaxis (hugging the wall that the paramecium arrives at after overshooting the turn), seems reasonable. For exploratory behavior in rats, a tedium theory has been proposed: the rat is satiated to one stimulus, causing it to be less likely to respond subsequently to the stimulus. For curiosity in rats and monkeys a titillation theory seems appropriate: the animals seek out novel stimuli. For monkeys and humans an innate need to know has been proposed. It is also true, however, that the kinds of behaviors investigators study in different species (or indeed, that the animals are capable of) get more and more complex as one moves up the phyletic scale; it may be that a more complex theory is needed to account for more complex behaviors.

Species differences in exploratory behavior are only now coming to light. The body of material in this area will undoubtedly become more complex and detailed in a few years. As an example, Neiberg et al. (1970) put hooded rats, Blue Gourami fish *(Trichogaster trichopterus sumatranus)*, and college students through two successive trials in a T-maze (the size of the mazes were adjusted for the different species!). The rats alternated the arm visited on the two trials, whereas the fish and the humans responded at the chance level. Cross-species comparisons are still rare, and many more species differences probably remain to be discovered.

References

Beach, F. A. 1947. Evolutionary changes in the physiological control of mating behavior in mammals. *Psychological Review* 54:297-315.

———. 1969. Locks and beagles. *American Psychologist* 24:971-89.

Berlyne, D. E. 1958. The influence of albedo and complexity of stimuli on visual fixation in the human infant. *British Journal of Psychology* 49:315-18.

Glickman, S. E.; and Sroges, R. W. 1966. Curiosity in zoo animals. *Behavior* (1966) 26:151-88.

Krechevsky, I. 1937. Brain mechanisms and variability. *Journal of Comparative Psychology* 23:139-63.

Lester, D. 1968. Response alternation. *Journal of Psychology* 69:131-42.

———. 1969. *Explorations in exploration*. New York: Van Nostrand Reinhold.

Lynn, R. 1966. *Attention, arousal, and the orientation reaction.* New York: Pergamon.

Maslow, A. H. 1954. *Motivation and personality.* New York: Harper & Row.

Mason, W. A.; and Harlow, H. F. 1959. Initial responses of infant monkeys to solid foods. *Psychological Reports* 5:193-99.

Neiberg, A.; Dale, J.; and Grainger, D. 1970. Alternation of stimulus and response in three species. *Psychonomic Science* 18:183-84.

Scott, J. P. 1961. Animal sexuality. In *Encyclopedia of sexual behavior,* ed. A. Ellis and A. Abarbanel, pp. 132-43. New York: Hawthorn.

Chapter 10

Social Behavior

SOCIAL BEHAVIOR is activity that is stimulated by or has some effect on other members of the same species. (Social behavior between members of different species is normally limited to predator-prey or parasite-host relationships and will not be discussed here.) Almost all animals have some social behavior in their repertoire, and almost all behavior can have some element of social causation.

As Hebb and Thompson (1969) have noted, the most elaborate social structures occur far apart in the phyletic scale, man's at the top and the social insects' near the bottom. In between, social groupings are loose and sporadic. Apart from the division of labor involved in sexual behavior and parental behavior, there are few cases in which subhuman vertebrates are dependent upon other members of the species for specialized functions that each does not have himself. Occasionally individual animals may act in a way that serves the whole group, but the service could be performed as well by other members of the species. There appears to be nothing in the behavior of gregarious mammals and birds that parallels the specification of function found in the social insects and in human society.

Some General Phyletic Trends

When we look at the various phyla in the animal kingdom, some general trends in the kinds of social organizations may be noted (Maier and Maier 1970). At the lowest end of the phyletic scale, one can find *aggregations* of animals of a species, groups of individual members of the species found close together because of the existence of favorable environmental conditions such as the presence of food. Such aggregations may often prove advantageous to the animals by increasing their chances of survival. For example, animals in aggregations often have a lower rate of respiration than isolated animals do. It is also found that toxic materials kill animals less quickly when their respiratory rate is low, so aggregation may increase the animals' resistance to toxic materials.

Several of the species in lower phyla form *colonial groups* in which the individuals are held together by morphological links. The most highly developed example of this is the Portuguese man-of-war, a jellyfish which consists of a colony of polyps, each having differentiated functions.

Caste systems are similar to colonial groups, in that members have specialized functions; but the functions differ because the members are not morphologically linked. The absence of morphological links is compensated for by the existence of a well-developed means of communication between members of the species. The best examples of a caste system are the insects and in particular, ants, termites, and bees.

Collective behavior is found primarily in vertebrates. Schools of fishes and formations of birds are good examples of this kind of social behavior, behavior which is based on allelomimetic behavioral systems (see below).

Other vertebrates, especially mammals, possess *dominance hierarchies,* in which the members of a group arrange themselves so that some members are dominant over others. Dominance procures certain privileges such as mating the female of choice, and eating first. Dominance hierarchies are found in many phyla. Among the arthropods, dominance hierarchies are found in some crabs (for example, the fiddler crab) and in some insects (for example, the cockroach). Dominance hierarchies are also found in fish and birds and in mammals such as cattle, wolves, and monkeys.

Behavioral Systems and Phyletic Trends

Scott (1969) argued that to study social behavior properly one must first make an inventory of the behavior patterns of animals. Closely related species may have similar behavior patterns for the same function (for example, barking in foxes, dogs, and wolves). Widely different species have different behavior patterns for the same function (sheep fight by backing off and running head-on, while goats rear up on their hind legs, throw their heads sideways, and clash as they come down).

Scott defined a behavioral system as several behavior patterns with a common function. The most common behavioral systems are:

> ingestive
> investigative
> shelter- or comfort-seeking
> sexual
> agonistic (fighting behavior)
> allelomimetic (contagious or imitative behavior)
> epimeletic (care-giving)
> et-epimeletic (care-soliciting)
> eliminative

Table 10.1 shows which of the behavioral systems are found in the different phyla.

131

TABLE 10.1.
Occurrence of behavioral systems in the animal kingdom.
From Scott 1969, p. 614.

Behavioral System

Phylum	shelter seeking	investi- gative	inges- tive	sex- ual	epime- letic	et-epi- meletic	allelo- mimetic	ago- nistic	elimi native
Protozoa	x	x	x	x	—	—	—	—	—
Porifera	—	—	—	—	—	—	—	—	—
Coelenterata	?	x	x	—	—	—	—	—	—
Echino- dermata	x	x	x	—	—	—	—	—	—
Platyhel- minthes	x	x	x	x	—	—	—	—	—
Nemathel- minthes	?	?	x	x	—	—	—	—	—
Annelida	?	x	x	x	—	—	—	—	—
Arthropoda	x	x	x	x	x	x	*	x	x
Mollusca	x	x	x	x	—	—	*	?	—
Chordata	x	x	x	x	x	x	x	x	x

* infrequent

Most of these behavioral systems can lead to social behavior. Shelter-seeking, investigative, and sexual behavior tend to produce temporary aggregations, as is common in invertebrates. Agonistic behavior tends to be dispersive in its effects and to prevent formation of groups unless behavior systems with cohesive effects are also present. Many groupings of vertebrates are based on allelomimetic behavioral systems. Nonvertebrate species lack the sense organs that permit continual contact and coordination with the movements of other individuals of the same species, and so rarely show allelomimetic behavior. Social groupings based on allelomimetic behavior are common in birds (formation flying) and fish (schooling); birds use vision for coordination, and fish use both vision and hearing.

Social groupings based on epimeletic and et-epimeletic behavioral systems tend to be long-lasting associations. Such social behavior is found only in arthropods and vertebrates.

In the arthropods, especially the insects, the social grouping is characterized by mutual feeding.

Scott noted that among the vertebrates, all kinds of social groupings are found. In some species, such as birds, social groupings may change seasonally, with flocking in winter and mated pairs in the spring. Scott argued that an additional factor is present in many vertebrates—primary bond formation. This arises as a result of *imprinting* and affects later social bonds made by the animal (such as the animal chosen for mating and the group joined). This primary bond, determining later social preference for animals similar to the parent, together with aggregation, could account for the social behavior that appears in animals of different species.

Some Specific Social Behaviors

So far in this chapter we have looked at large changes in social behavior in general across different phyla. For some social behaviors a more detailed comparative analysis is possible. We will consider two behaviors here that have been studied extensively from a comparative point of view, imprinting and altruism.

Imprinting

About 1900 it was noted that birds become attached to objects that are present during a "critical period" of their development. For example, if a pigeon is hatched by the adult of a different species of pigeon, the bird will prefer mates of the same species as its foster parent. Lorenz (1952) noted that if he was present during this critical period (which for birds may fall during the first day after hatching), the bird would "imprint" upon him. Lorenz felt that the first object

133

to elicit a social response in the bird later released not only that response but also related responses such as sexual behavior.

The phenomenon of imprinting shows some phyletic trends. Imprinting has been demonstrated in birds, insects, fish, and in some mammals such as sheep, deer, and buffalo. It seems that in general, imprinting is found in precocial animal species and not altricial species, that is, where the newborn are mobile almost immediately after birth and not where there is a prolonged helpless infancy.

It has been claimed that imprinting effects can be demonstrated in monkeys as well as humans. However, in altricial animals whose behavioral repertoire is quite limited for a long time after birth, it is difficult to distinguish between the specific phenomenon of imprinting and the general effects of early learning. One of the defining features of imprinting is that there is a critical period during which social contacts produce a lasting behavioral change. Scott (1969) noted that perhaps the critical period gets longer with the phyletically more complex species and that the critical period does not appear so soon after birth. Clearly a critical period that extends for weeks is not as "critical" as one that extends for a few hours (as in ducklings), so we may well be dealing with different phenomena if we compare smiling in the human infant with the following response in ducklings. On the other hand, it may prove impossible to distinguish between imprinting and general early learning, in which case the phyletic trends noted by Scott may be valid.

Hess (1959) has summarized his experiences with imprinting different species and has rated the animals according to the ease with which they can be imprinted:

ducks:	wild mallard	E+
	domesticated mallard	E
	Peking	G
	Rouen	F
	wood	P
	black	G

geese:	Canada	E+
	pilgrim	G
chickens:	jungle fowl	G
	Cochin bantam	G
	New Hampshire red	G
	Rhode Island red	G
	barred rock	G
	Vantress broiler	G+
	white rock	F
	leghorn	P
other fowl:	pheasant	P
	Eastern bobwhite quail	G
	California valley quail	E
	turkey	F
mammals:	sheep	G
	guinea pig	G

(E=excellent, G=good, F=fair, P=poor)

Altruism

Hebb and Thompson (1969) defined three levels of cooperation: (1) reflexive or nonpurposive (for example, a bird's regurgitation of food when a chick puts its beak down the parent's throat), (2) purposive but one-sided (human care of young infants), and (3) two-sided work or teamwork (playing a game). They felt that level 2 appeared only in the higher vertebrates (the apes and above, primarily) and that level 3 appears only in man. Hebb and Thompson noted that the word "purposive" did not imply that the response had biological significance, but that it was intended by the animal which had some awareness of the consequences of the response.

Hebb and Thompson felt that there was evidence of a phyletic trend in altruism, that is, behavior which is not reflexive or immediately rewarding biologically, but rather entails a nondestructive interest in others. They felt that altruism was manifest in maternal care (at a purposive level), in the long-term attachment of sexual partners and in selective friend-

135

ships that are not dependent on primary reinforcement (as found in dogs, chimpanzees, and porpoises).

Krebs (1970) reviewed the experimental literature on altruism in animals, however, and concluded that there is no evidence for altruism in the two species he studied, rats and chimpanzees. Though rats have been found to press a bar, which has the effect of removing a struggling rat from a tank of water, Krebs argued that there was a negative reinforcer at work here—the reduction in noise made by the struggling rat. Krebs felt that the examples given by Hebb and Thompson were anecdotal rather than the results of controlled studies.

Part of the problem here involves the difficulty of defining "altruism" adequately. It is noteworthy that biologists use the term more broadly than do experimental psychologists. For example, Brown (1970) saw cooperative breeding (communal participation of the members of a social group in the various activities essential to successful reproduction and recruitment in the group) as altruistic behavior. Brown adopted the definition of altruism proposed by Hamilton (1963)—the sacrificing of an individual's own fitness to enhance the fitness of other individuals, with no implications for the emotional and cognitive state of the animal or the neural mechanisms at work.

The Importance of the Range of Species Studied

It should be noted that the conclusions drawn from a survey of several species may depend crucially on the species that are compared. In studying social behavior, interphylum differences are more easily described than intraphylum differences. For example, looking primarily at vertebrate species, Thompson (1958) found few phyletic trends in the size and density of social groupings of different species, that is, the number of individuals in a group and their distribution over a locale.

He concluded that either there were no trends or the trends were very complex and have eluded his inspection of the data. Similarly, he found no phyletic trends in the cohesiveness of members of a species or in the syntality of the members (that is, the degree to which the members of a group act as a unit in the achievement of goals). With regard to the stability of individual relationships, Thompson noted that in general phyletically higher species have more stable relationships (partly due to the presence of dominance hierarchies and emotional interactions). Thus, for example, bird and mammalian groups are more stable than groups of fish and lizards. However, the variability among vertebrates is sufficiently large that groupings of varying degrees of stability can be found. Finally, Thompson noted that there appeared to be no phyletic trend in the permeability of social groupings, that is, the degree to which members of a group permit the intrusion of strange individuals.

Scott (1969) drew a similar conclusion about phyletic differences in the social behavior of the primates. The individual species differ greatly, and a variety of social arrangements can be found—one male with a harem, several males combining their strength to head a group, etc.

On the other hand, in looking at interphyla differences, as we did in this chapter when we discussed the views of Maier and Maier and of Scott, phyletic trends can be noted. It appears, therefore, that the range of species investigated may crucially affect the conclusions drawn. If the range investigated is small, no trends may be observed.

References

Brown, J. L. 1970. Cooperative breeding and altruistic behavior in the Mexican jay, Aphelocoma ultramarina. *Animal Behavior* 18:366-78.
Hamilton, W. D. 1963. The evolution of altruistic behavior. *American Naturalist* 97:354-56.

Hebb, D. O.; and Thompson, W. R. 1969. The social significance of animal studies. In *The Handbook of social psychology,* vol. 2, ed. G. Lindzey and E. Aronson, pp. 729-74. Reading, Mass.: Addison-Wesley.

Hess, E. H. 1959. Imprinting. *Science* 130:133-41.

Krebs, D. L. 1970. Altruism. *Psychological Bulletin* 73:258-302.

Lorenz, K. 1952. *King Solomon's ring.* New York: Crowell.

Maier, R. A.; and Maier, B. M. 1970. *Comparative animal behavior.* Belmont, Cal.: Brooks/Cole.

Scott, J. P. 1969. The social psychology of infrahuman animals. In *The handbook of social psychology,* vol. 1, ed. G. Lindzey and E. Aronson, pp. 611-42. Reading, Mass.: Addison-Wesley.

Thompson, W. R. 1958. Social behavior. In *Behavior and evolution,* ed. A. Roe and G. G. Simpson, pp. 291-310. New Haven: Yale Univ. Press.

Chapter 11

Abnormal Behavior

WHEN AN OBSERVER becomes acquainted with a species of animals, he soon begins to be able to distinguish the different "personalities" of the animals. There has been little formal investigation of these within-species differences; similarly, little has been done on between-species differences. (There are a few exceptions to the latter statement. Glickman and Hartz [1964] studied exploratory behavior in several species of rodents; their data enable the species to be classified in the dimension of timidity.) However, although animal "personality" has not been studied, some work has been done on the abnormal aspects of animal behavior. These phenomena may be comparable to emotional disturbance in man. The work that has been done is quite scarce, so this chapter will have the appearance of a short compilation rather than an integrated survey.

The Varieties of Abnormal Behavior

There are reports of abnormal behavior occurring in animals, which resemble abnormal behavior in man. Fox (1968a) has reported examples of depression, hysteria, epilepsy, neurotic behavior, and psychopathic behavior in animals, and Fox (1968b) and Brunner (1968) have reported syndromes in animals that appear to resemble schizophrenia and autism. Schmidt (1968) reported examples of anorexia nervosa and psychosomatic disorders such as gastrointestinal ulcers, alopecia, and eczema. Meyer-Holzapfel (1968) has reported examples of stereotyped behavior in zoo animals, such as weaving motions and stereotyped walking patterns. There are also reports of experimentally induced alcohol addiction in cats (Masserman and Yum 1946) and morphine addiction in mice (Maggiolo and Huidobro 1961).

It would seem that many abnormal behaviors similar to those found in man can be induced in animals and may sometimes occur without experimental manipulation. Not much systematic research has been conducted in these aspects of behavior; certainly there are no comparative studies. It is noteworthy that all of the examples reported are in mammals, mainly monkeys, dogs, cats, ungulates, and rodents. This may be a result of the fact that by *abnormal behavior* we mean behavior that resembles abnormal behavior in man. Abnormal behavior defined relative to each species would be more difficult to study. How would we recognize abnormal behavior in an insect or a flatworm?

Animal Hypnosis

The term *hypnotic state* is generally used to describe a condition in which a human being seems to lose control of volition and to behave in unusual ways at the behest of another person. Some authorities (Barber 1969) doubt that there is any such condition which cannot be duplicated in the absence of a "hypnotic" procedure, but they do not deny that many human beings behave abnormally after submitting to particular procedures.

So-called hypnotic states can be induced in many species of animals (Chertok 1968). Various techniques have been used: placing the animal in a supine position, fixing its gaze, grasping it suddenly, hooding birds (as in falconry). The animal is left in a cataleptic state, motionless and unresponsive. Certain natural phenomena also appear to be akin to these hypnotic states. Mayer's stick insect *(Haplopus mayeri)* is active at dawn but falls into a cataleptic state for the rest of the day. Some fish enter this state when removed from water. Some animals become motionless at the sight of others; for example, the possum *(Didelphis virginicus)* spontaneously falls into catalepsy at the sight of snakes.

This is not the place to discuss various theories that have been proposed for the phenomenon of hypnosis in animals. We may note, however, that the importance of psychological factors in producing hypnotic states appears to be greater in animals higher in the phyletic scale. In man and the higher animals experimental hypnosis can be induced through psychical inhibition (by altering the normal course of their interchange or communication). In mammals, birds, reptiles, amphibians, crustaceans, and insects, experimental hypnosis can be induced through mechanical inhibition (such as immobilization). In crustaceans and insects, natural hypnosis occurs.

Grief and Mourning

Most of the symptoms typically observed in grieving humans have been observed in other animals. The death of a mate or child, or separation from a companion, leads to behaviors such as restlessness, apathy, withdrawal, aggression directed toward self and others, a loss of appetite and sexual interest, an inability to establish new relationships, and so on (Averill 1968). However, most of the data here are anecdotal, and there are no comparative studies in the literature.

Reviews of the anecdotal material (Pollock 1961) indicate that components of the grief reaction have been observed in dogs, sheep, cats, monkeys, and the higher primates. Bowlby (1961) also reported anecdotal material on grief reactions in birds (jackdaws and geese). Grief reactions have not been reported in reptiles, amphibians, or fish.

Bowlby noted that the grief reactions in animals tend to be more transient (of shorter duration) than reactions of grief in man. He also felt that self-directed hostility was absent in animals, although there have been reports in monkeys of self-mutilation resulting from loss (Tinklepaugh 1928). Bowlby also felt that identification with the lost object was a feature only of human grief and mourning.

Incidentally, although tearing (watering) of the eyes can occur in many species of animals, Montagu (1959) asserts that psychic weeping (shedding tears when distressed) is characteristic only of man. He notes that psychic weeping appears to be a late development, both phylogenetically and ontogenetically, for tearing does not appear in infants until about six weeks of age.

Do Animals Commit Suicide?

The debate as to whether animals kill themselves has been in progress for many years. Certainly some animals do die under circumstances in which a suicidal death would be suspected were the animal a human. The most famous anecdotal example is that of the Norwegian lemming, which migrates twice every year between its winter and summer habitats. This migration, coupled with the fact that the lemming population goes through drastic changes in numbers, has led to tales (largely unsubstantiated) of lemming migrations in which, rather than turn from their path, lemmings drown in rivers or jump off cliffs to their deaths.

In the past the debate has usually been decided by opinion

backed up by a writer's professional reputation. Goldstein (1940) asserts that animals do not commit suicide. In his opinion, suicide is a conscious and rational act; a person willingly chooses death as a solution to his problems. Animals, on the other hand, are clearly not capable of conscious and rational choices and so cannot kill themselves. Neither, for that matter, can humans with severe brain injuries, except during rare, lucid moments. If animals die, no matter how closely the death resembles a human suicide, the death is a mere accident.

In contrast, Menninger (1938) asserts that animals *can* commit suicide. He feels that suicidal motivation can operate at an unconscious level and sees many self-destructive behaviors as being partially determined by suicidal motivation, for example, alcoholism and self-mutilation. There is abundant evidence that animals can show this kind of self-destructive behavior. Masserman and Yum (1946), by providing ethanol to drink when animals were under stress, produced cats that were alcoholics. Harlow and Harlow (1962) have found that raising monkeys in isolation results in animals that mutilate themselves.

Recently, some anecdotal evidence has appeared which suggests that dolphins can commit suicide. John Lilly (see Amory 1970) has reported that, if dolphins are allowed to become attached to one person who then leaves, they frequently die. Since the dolphin is considered to be one of the most intelligent animals and since this sequence of events suggests perhaps that the dolphins were mourning the loss of their companions, the idea that their deaths were suicidal is hard to resist.

Anecdotal evidence, however, can never convince the skeptic. It is never more than suggestive. Similarly, ex cathedra statements from people, however famous, are not convincing. What is needed is a way of proving that animals do or do not, on occasion, kill themselves.

This task has been attacked by Schaefer (1967) in a way that may provide an answer to the debate. Schaefer identified the basic criteria for deciding whether an animal can commit suicide: (1) the animal must be able to distinguish between life and death, or, to be more specific, between a live animal and a dead one; (2) it must be able to distinguish between a lethal chamber and a nonlethal chamber; and (3) under certain circumstances it must choose to enter the lethal chamber.

Schaefer demonstrated that a mouse can distinguish between a live mouse and a dead mouse by placing the subject in a box with an observation room. When another live mouse was in the observation room a lever in the subject's box produced food when pressed. When a dead mouse was in the observation room, the lever did not produce food when pressed. The experimental mice indicated by their frequency of lever pressing that they could learn this discrimination.

But some of Schaefer's colleagues have objected to this demonstration. The mouse they say, is learning to distinguish only between moving and nonmoving mice, not between live and dead mice. But as Schaefer noted, movement—or the lack of it—is the predominant cue humans use to decide whether someone is dead. Why belittle the mouse for using the same cue?

Can a mouse learn to discriminate between a lethal and a nonlethal chamber? To demonstrate that it can, Schaefer again allowed the subject mouse to learn from watching his conspecifics. Mice were introduced one at a time into a two-choice maze. If the mice entered chamber A they were instantly electrocuted. If they entered chamber B they were allowed to live. As long as the mouse was alive, one lever in the box containing the subject mouse produced food. When the mouse was dead, a different lever produced food. The subject mice learned this discrimination. Schaefer then allowed the subject mice to choose one of the two chambers to enter. On all trials the subject mice chose to enter the nonlethal chamber.

Obviously Schaefer's demonstrations do not yet prove that a mouse could commit suicide. It would be necessary to see whether a mouse could learn to discriminate between a dead mouse and a sleeping mouse. In the second demonstration, perhaps it is the change of state of the observed mouse that causes the subject mouse to avoid the lethal chamber. Perhaps it would avoid the chamber if an anesthetized mouse suddenly woke up in it. There are many such factors to control for.

If the demonstrations *were* to provide evidence that an animal can discriminate between live animals and a dead animal and between a lethal and a nonlethal chamber, then we could determine under what circumstances an animal would choose to enter the lethal chamber.

It appears that the answer to the question of whether an animal can commit suicide is still "perhaps," but we now have a technique that may help to answer the question.

Zoos and Mental Hospitals

In the final section of this chapter on abnormal behavior, we will look at the similarities in the behavior of patients in psychiatric hospitals and at animals in zoos. It is impressive that the two kinds of situations produce similar reactions among their inhabitants.

Ellenberger (1960) notes that patients in mental hospitals often have psychopathological reactions, neurotic reactions, psychotic reactions, and psychopathic reactions merely as a result of being in the hospital. In the extreme, the patients show severe emotional regression and infantilism. Similar trends are occasionally found in the staff of the mental hospital. Such reactions are less common in situations where there is an intensive therapy program.

Ellenberger notes that these reactions have been found in monasteries (where the reactions were reduced by the occupational therapy introduced by St. Benedict in the fifth century A.D.), prisons, TB sanatoriums, hospitals, orphanages, and old folks' homes. Similar reactions have also been observed among animals in zoos.

145

Ellenberger identified four main reactions found in zoo animals and psychiatric patients, which result simply from being confined:

1. *Trauma of captivity*. When captured and placed in a zoo, an animal is deprived of its territory. It cannot flee enemies or attack them. This can lead to anxiety, feverish activity, stereotyped movements, and self-mutilation or to stupor and refusal to eat. The reaction is more severe in older animals. A similar reaction is found in psychiatric patients. Ellenberger particularly cites cases in which the commitment of a person to a mental hospital was made without the individual's permission or awareness. One man was sedated without his knowledge and then transported 1,400 miles to a mental hospital. His relatives then went home. Such a commitment is much like the capture of a wild animal.

2. *Nesting process*. When placed in its cage the zoo animal eventually establishes its territory in the space allowed. After this, the animal can be offered an opportunity to escape, but will not. It will most likely return to its cage if allowed to. (Barriers in a zoo are mainly to protect the animals from the public rather than the public from the animals.) When an animal escapes from a zoo, it resembles a displaced person trying to get home rather than a prisoner regaining his liberty. Similar behavior is found among psychiatric patients; they take roots in the hospital, establish a place, and can be reluctant to leave.

3. *Syndromes produced by social competition and frustration*. Social rank is very important in animal societies. If the ranking is upset, a colony of animals may fight and the colony may be quickly reduced to a few animals. Social rank and pecking orders tend to be stricter and more despotic among zoo animals than among wild animals, which may be due to the fact that escape and flight are not available to them. A second source of competition is from favoritism, from both zoo keepers and the public. An animal that is not a favorite will often be upset by its relative neglect. Similar phenomena are found in psychiatric patients. Social ranking tends to be

more obvious and more important, but patients are distressed by favoritism on the part of the staff toward others.

4. *Emotional deterioration*. Animals in zoos, as well as psychiatric patients, often show emotional deterioration as a result of their confinement—depression, stereotypic movements (bears nod their heads, hyenas walk in sterotyped paths), coprophagia, and so forth.

In these four respects, therefore, zoo animals and psychiatric patients show similarities in their behavior, behavior resulting solely from confinement.

Incidentally, Ellenberger noted a curious reversal of roles for zoos and mental hospitals. Several hundred years ago, zoos were set up by rich people for their own enjoyment. They were private; the public was not allowed in. But until modern times, mental asylums were open to the public; Bethlehem Hospital (Bedlam) in London used to receive up to 300 visitors a day. The public came to see the patients and were allowed to talk to them, often bringing them gifts (such as liquor). The asylums had their "star attractions," usually the manic-depressive patients in manic states. In the course of time, these roles have been reversed; today it is the mental hospital that is private and the zoo that is public.

References

Amory, C. 1970. After living with man, a dolphin may commit suicide. *Holiday* May:16-18.

Averill, J. R. 1968. Grief. *Psychological Bulletin* 70:721-48.

Barber, T. X. 1969. *Hypnosis*. Princeton: Van Nostrand.

Bowlby, J. 1961. Processes of mourning. *International Journal of Psychoanalysis* 42:317-40.

Brunner, F. 1968. The application of behavior studies in small animal practice. In *Abnormal behavior in animals,* ed. M. W. Fox, pp. 398-449. Philadelphia: Saunders.

Chertok, L. 1968. Animal hypnosis. In *Abnormal behavior in animals,* ed. M. W. Fox, pp. 129-58. Philadelphia: Saunders.

Ellenberger, H. F. 1960. Zoological garden and mental hospital. *Canadian Psychiatric Association Journal* 5:136-49.

Fox, M. W., ed. 1968. *Abnormal behavior in animals*. Philadelphia: Saunders.

————. 1968a. Socialization, environmental factors, and abnormal behavior development in animals. In *Abnormal behavior in animals,* ed. M. W. Fox, pp. 332-55. Philadelphia: Saunders.

————. 1968b. Psychomotor disturbances. In *Abnormal behavior in animals,* ed. M. W. Fox, pp. 356-64. Philadelphia: Saunders.

Glickman, S. E.; and Hartz, K. E. 1964. Exploratory behavior in several species of rodents. *Journal of Comparative and Physiological Psychology* 58:101-104.

Goldstein, K. 1940. *Human nature in the light of psychopathology.* Cambridge, Mass.: Harvard Univ. Press.

Harlow, H. F.; and Harlow, M. K. 1962. Social deprivation in monkeys. *Scientific American* 207(5):136-46.

Maggiolo, C.; and Huidobro, F. 1961. Administration of pellets of morphine to mice. *Acta Physiologica Latinoamerica* 11:70-78.

Masserman, J. H.; and Yum, K. S. 1946. An analysis of the influence of alcohol in experimental neuroses in cats. *Psychosomatic Medicine* 8:36-52.

Menninger, K. 1938. *Man against himself.* New York: Harcourt, Brace & World.

Meyer-Holzapfel, M. 1968. Abnormal behavior in zoo animals. In *Abnormal behavior in animals,* ed. M. W. Fox, pp. 476-503. Philadelphia: Saunders.

Montagu, A. 1959. Natural selection and the origin and evolution of weeping in man. *Science* 130:1,572-73.

Pollock, G. H. 1961. Mourning and adaptation. *International Journal of Psychoanalysis* 42:341-61.

Schaefer, H. H. 1967. Can a mouse commit suicide? In *Essays in self-destruction,* ed. E. S. Shneidman, pp. 494-509. New York: Science House.

Tinklepaugh, O. L. 1928. The self-mutilation of a male Macacus rhesus monkey. *Journal of Mammalology* 9:293-300.

Chapter 12

Communication

THE WAYS in which animals communicate with one another depends overwhelmingly on the senses they develop. Thus the means of communication closely parallels the degree of sensitivity of the different senses in an animal (see Chap. 6). We can find examples of all the senses being used in communication by one species or another.

The chemical senses are commonly used by animals. Most mammals have a highly developed olfactory sense, which is used for social communication (Ralls 1971). Common chemical signals utilize urine, feces, and excretions from the cutaneous scent glands. Scent marking is utilized by animals to indicate their territory; marking is especially common when the animal is dominant and likely to attack intruders (particularly if it is likely to win any fight that ensues). Chemical communication is frequently a way of attracting members of the opposite sex or of notifying them of the presence of a potential mate. It has been noted in species as different from one another as the gypsy moth and the rhesus monkey (Michael et al. 1971).

Gestures and motor movements are commonly employed for communication between members of a species. The honey bee returning to the hive after finding nectar performs a dance in which the pattern and speed of the movements indicate the direction and distance of the nectar (Gould et al. 1970). Fox (1970) has explored the facial expressions of canids and notes consistent expressions used in association with clearly definable stimulus situations such as "intention to bite" and "about to flee." Similar repertoires of expressions may be found in primates.

Auditory communication is also common and is illustrated by the song of birds, the grunts and shrieks of primates, and the speech of humans.

Different species rely on different senses for communication, but this varying reliance seems related to the development of the specific sensory structures. Phyletic trends are therefore rarely found between species. Thus there is little to be gained here in detailing the various methods by which members of different species communicate with one another.

Aside from the study of the *method* of communication, the most commonly studied quality is the complexity of communication. Here we occasionally find general trends identified. For example, Fox (1970), in his study of the facial expressions of canids, felt that the complexity of the repertoire is related to the degree of the social organization of species. Those expressions found in solitary species of canids (such as the red fox) develop early in the life of a gregarious species (such as the wolf), but gregarious species develop additional patterns of facial expression which can be integrated into more elaborate expressions not found in the solitary canids. Fox suggests that the facial expressions that develop first in the social species of canids are "ancestral" patterns, which is to say that they are phylogenetically simpler and that they are eventually superseded by more recently evolved patterns. It should be noted here that Fox's analysis points to a commonly held maxim in biology, namely, that phylogeny parallels ontogeny (discussed in Chapter 3).

The complexity of communication in man is apparently unequalled by that of any other species. In fact, we might say that, though many animals have communication, only man is known to communicate in a way that amounts to language. Language involves a flexible system of symbols which can be combined in different ways and which have different meanings depending on context. The communication of subhumans generally involves a fixed meaning for each cry or posture.

Attempts were made earlier this century to determine whether chimpanzees might be taught to speak. If this had been accomplished, the apparent gap between other animals and man would seem reduced. However, the attempts were quite unsuccessful. For example, one of the chimpanzees managed to acquire a vocabulary of a few words, but only with a great deal of difficulty (Kellogg 1968).

Recently, Gardner and Gardner (1969) hit upon the idea of teaching a chimpanzee the sign language used by the deaf and dumb, rather than the vocal language used by normal men. By working intensively with a young female chimpanzee named "Washoe," they enabled her to acquire a vocabulary of over 50 words. The complexity of the communications made by Washoe can be illustrated by the following sample. Emily Hahn visited Washoe and watched her playing on an island with other chimpanzees. Washoe spied Emily and a friend (Roger) drinking iced tea on the mainland and she left her companions, hurried to the bank of the island, and began gesturing furiously. Roughly translated:

> She begged and begged Roger to come and fetch her. She kept signing, "Roger ride come gimme sweet eat please hurry hurry you come please gimme sweet you hurry you come ride Roger come give Washoe fruit drink hurry hurry fruit drink sweet please please". . . . (Just then a plane flew overhead, and Washoe signed) "You me ride in plane." (Hahn 1971, p. 98.)

Such an ability brings home Harlow's point (Harlow 1958; see Chap. 8), that a relatively small intellectual gain could make possible the development of symbolic language and culture. The great gulf in this respect between man and other animals seems less now because of Washoe's feat.

References

Fox, M. W. 1970. A comparative study of the development of facial expressions in canids. *Behavior* 36:49-73.

Gardner, R. A.; and Gardner, B. T. 1969. Teaching sign language to a chimpanzee. *Science* 165:664-72.

Gould, J. L.; Henerey, M.; and MacLeod, M. C. 1970. Communication of direction by the honey bee. *Science* 169:544-54.

Hahn, E. 1971. A reporter at large. *The New Yorker* 47:#43 (Dec. 11) 54-98.

Harlow, H. 1958. The evolution of learning. In *Behavior and evolution,* ed. A. Roe and G. G. Simpson, pp. 269-90. New Haven: Yale Univ. Press.

Kellogg, W. N. 1968. Communication and language in the home-raised chimpanzee. *Science* 168:423-27.

Michael, R. P.; Keverne, E. B.; and Bonsall, R. W. 1971. Pheromones. *Science* 172:964-66.

Ralls, K. 1971. Mammalian scent marking. *Science* 171:443-49.

IV
Theoretical Issues

Chapter 13

Criticisms of Comparative Psychology

THERE HAVE BEEN many attacks on compara-
tive psychology. They have varied in their aim, some involving
the methods used to study animal behavior by comparative
psychologists, while others criticized the explicit and implicit
principles used to interpret the results of the studies. In this
chapter we will review some unfavorable analyses of comparative psychological work, as well as some of the suggestions for
improvement made by critics. The major criticisms discussed
will be (1) those of the ethologists, (2) those involving the use
of the phylogenetic scale, and (3) those which call the existence
of comparative psychology itself into question.

Ethology and Comparative Psychology

During the 1950s and part of the 1960s, there was considerable disagreement between the ethologists and the comparative
psychologists on the topic of animal behavior. It is appropriate,

therefore, that some mention be made here of the issues involved, though to a large extent the argument has died down in recent years.

Most of the comparative psychologists are Americans and of course were trained primarily as psychologists. They had been educated in a manner which stresses the importance of taking animals into the laboratory, simplifying the experimental situation down to its bare essentials, and designing studies in which one variable at a time is manipulated, while the experimenter endeavors to hold other variables constant. Comparative psychologists have designed such apparatus as the T-maze, Skinner box, Lashley jumping stand, and shuttle box. With this apparatus the behavior of interest can be studied simply and with a minimum of subjectivity and inference.

Meanwhile, the ethologists are generally European and were trained primarily as zoologists. They prefer to study animals in their natural settings and to interfere as little as possible in the natural behavior of the animal. Thus, although ethologists are by no means opposed to experimental research, much of their data consist of nonexperimental observation. Therefore, to some psychologists, ethological work has been tainted by the inclusion of subjective data.

One result of these two approaches is that the comparative psychologists have primarily studied laboratory animals, species bred specifically for traits that would be useful in laboratory work and for genetic homogeneity. This has often restricted their work to a few species, notably the rat, mouse, cat, and dog. The ethologists, on the other hand, have studied all kinds of animals rather than those bred especially for research. Occasionally animals might be tamed for closer study, but they were not inbred or selected for special characteristics. The ethologists' studies were probably also affected by the fact that they frequently chose birds as subjects. Birds often have stereotyped behaviors which can be expected to occur after particular kinds of stimulation; such behaviors have assumed an important role in ethological theory.

The Nature-Nurture Issue

These differences in themselves might not have led to serious disagreement. The catalyst was the different explanations each group proposed for animal behavior.

The ethologists adopted a stance that stressed the role of innate factors. They rehabilitated the concept of *instinct* and applied it to animal behavior. An *instinct* for the ethologist meant an inherited, specific, stereotyped pattern of behavior. It had its own source of energy and was released, rather than guided, by environmental stimuli. Some ethologists used the term instinct to refer to the consummatory or terminal phase of the behavior pattern, and used the term *instinctive behavior* to refer to the active sequence of behavior.

Unfortunately, the concept of instinct had fallen into disrepute in American psychology, chiefly because it had been abused. Psychologists in the early part of this century had too often proposed a new instinct in order to account for a particular behavior, so that Bernard (1924) was able to catalogue several thousand instincts that had been proposed by someone or other to account for behavior. Such misuse caused the concept to lose any exploratory value it might otherwise have had.

Furthermore, American psychologists were profoundly influenced by the views of Watson (1924) who adopted the point of view that learning was most crucial in the determination of behavior. In response to the ethologists, various psychologists (for example, Lehrman 1953) undertook to show how particular behaviors were influenced by the experiences undergone by an animal. (Even isolating the animal does not isolate it from its own self; it may be able to learn from feedback from its own behavior.)

The nature-nurture controversy in psychology is a long-standing one. In spite of frequent announcements that it is a dead issue (Hebb 1953), it frequently raises its head and polarizes researchers even today. Nature and nurture interact to determine behavior, and it is often difficult to separate their individual contributions. Furthermore, since inherited factors are affected by the environment and learned factors are affected by genetic inheritance, it is often logically impossible to separate their influences. As Lehrman (1953) argued, the crucial task is to identify the processes and mechanisms involved in producing the behavior, rather than arguing which of two arbitrarily dichotomized factors is chiefly responsible.

The Laboratory and the Field

Although laboratory researchers and field researchers tend to utilize different settings for their studies, the differences involved in the studies need not be great. Naturalistic research can meet the same rigorous methodological standards as laboratory research (Willems and Raush 1969). It must be admitted, though, that ethologists have sometimes tended toward an uncritical use of anecdotal and inferential data, which has sometimes led them into errors.* Like experimental studies, naturalistic studies need to be replicated rather than simply accepted.

In a meaningful examination of phyletic differences in animal behavior, however, both kinds of research play an important role. For example, in determining how well an animal can perform a particular task, we often have to choose a task that is "meaningful" for the animal, a decision which must be made on the basis of field observation. The particular test of an ability may differ considerably for different species. As an illustration, the toad often performs quite poorly in tests of avoidance learning in shuttle boxes (Boice 1970), whereas Brower and Brower (1962) have shown that toads

---

* For example, Lorenz (1966), who helped provide the impetus for ethological research, has fallen into this error. He described the submission gesture of the wolf in defeat and noted that the defeated wolf bares its throat to the victor. Scott (1970) pointed out that it is in fact the victorious wolf that turns its head away, thereby baring its throat to the defeated wolf. Errors such as this makes some investigators distrust much of what the ethologists conclude.

learn—in one trial—which insects will sting them when eaten.

On the other hand, when we are interested in quantitative differences inabilities, it is often necessary to use a standardized task. For example, if we want to compare the speed of learning, it often makes sense to place all animals in the same situation (a T-maze or a Skinner box) so that the data are more comparable.

The two approaches, while different, are not contradictory. They should be viewed as complementary. As Menzel has said (in Willems and Rausch 1969), ". . . the field worker and the laboratory man, insofar as they are scientific organizers of data rather than cataloguers or technicians, tend to adopt different but compatible methods of achieving perspective. The methods are analogous to *zooming in* and *zooming out* with a lens. To the extent that they are reproduced objectively, wide-angle, telephoto, and microscopic views must be *simultaneously* valid, and zooming from different directions simply focuses attention on different facets of the same phenomenon. We must try to achieve both generality and detail, and if possible, do this under a single set of principles. . . . [p. 82] I see neither halos nor horns on either a *real experiment* or on *accurate observations*. Any method is a special case of human experience, and it cannot surpass the limitations of its human interpreters." [p. 80]

Although the controversy between ethologists and comparative psychologists generated much heat, much dialogue, and a good deal of research, the argument does not concern us much in this book, since the topics they fought about (such as the role of innate factors in the determination of behavior) have not contributed significantly to the comparative data that we have discussed. For a good unbiased review of the disagreement, the reader is referred to Cofer and Apley (1964).

The Myth of the Phylogenetic Scale

Hodos and Campbell (1969) have recently advanced a seri-   159 ous criticism of comparative psychology as it exists today. They point out that the species chosen for comparison are selected arbitrarily and without any goal other than comparison for the sake of comparison. There appears to be an absence of any theoretical foundation for the field, except perhaps the implicit assumption that animals are arranged according to the phylogenetic scale. In criticizing comparative psychologists, Hodos and Campbell focused on several major problem areas.

The Phylogenetic Scale

Aristotle tried out various schemes for classifying animals—by the number of legs, whether they possessed blood, and so on. Later scholars took his work and extended it to produce a ranking of animals in which every animal could be ranked on the same dimension, known as the *scala naturae*. The lowest position on this scale was occupied by the sponges and other animals considered formless. At the top of the scale was man or, after the infusion of religious thought into the topic, God. This "great chain of being" was very important in medieval thought.

Such a scale is an attractive idea. The phylogenetic scale appears to be the modern counterpart of the *scala naturae*. Animals are designated as subprimates, or lower animals, as if the animals could really be ordered on one dimension. In fact, there is no such single scale. It is impossible to decide whether a porpoise is higher or lower than a cat, for example, since it may be higher in one dimension and lower in another. In view of the fact that there is no single phylogenetic scale, Hodos and Campbell urge that terms like *subprimate* be dropped from use and replaced by a term such as *nonprimate*.

There is, albeit in a very tentative way, an organization of animal species based on probable lines of descent—the phylogenetic tree (see Fig. 13.1). This organization is continually open to modification as new data are acquired. If the

160

phylogenetic tree is used as a basis for classifying animals, it becomes meaningless to make the statement that amphibians, for example, represent a higher degree of evolutionary development than do teleost fishes, since each of these animals has followed an independent course of evolution.

Using the concept of the phylogenetic tree, let us say that man is no longer at the highest point, or indeed special in any way. He is merely one of the many species that has evolved and survives today. It is interesting that when a phylogenetic tree is drawn, the branching of the tree is so arranged that man comes at one of the extreme ends of the tree. Man himself, not scientific knowledge, gives him this unique place.

As one considers the phylogenetic tree, some interesting facts emerge. For example, carnivores and rodents are often compared with primates, yet each has followed an independent line of evolution from the primates and from each other since the late Cretaceous period. The rat was never an ancestor of the cat nor the cat of the monkey. A comparison of rat-cat-monkey, therefore, does not tell us anything about phylogenesis.

Some phylogenetic sequences can be guessed. For example, the early primates appear to have developed from the insectivores; the living prosimians (tarsiers, lorises, and lemurs) retain some insectivore characteristics. A comparison of living insectivores, prosimians, Old World monkeys, apes, and man would give some clues to the evolutionary trends in the development of man.

One of the major problems in this kind of analysis is the identification of one representative or a group of animals that can be assumed to represent the (now extinct) ancestor. The modern insectivore, for example, may have evolved considerably from the ancestral insectivore from which the early prosimians developed. Decisions are made with difficulty, because fossils can tell us little about the central nervous system or the behavior of the ancestors other than what can be inferred from the fossilized morphological characteristics.

It is often incorrect to choose a "primitive animal" as

161

a representative of the ancestral form, for simplicity may be a product of evolution. One trait may be primitive in one species and the product of evolutionary specialization in another. In fact, Hodos (1970) recommends the use of "ancestral" rather than "primitive" in descriptions of animals and their characteristics and of the term "derived character" rather than "specialized."

One guide that Hodos and Campbell suggested was that animals that are morphologically ancestral are likely to resemble the ancestral form in behavior, and those animals that have derived morphological characters are likely to have derived behavioral characters. (The older terminology was simpler, though incorrect!)

Considerations such as these point to crucial animals for study. For example, the hedgehog probably resembles the ancestral insectivores most closely of all living insectivores and therefore is worthy of close study. Similarly, the monotremes (for example, the duck-billed platypus) are important because of their resemblance to primitive mammals. We can expect the writings of Hodos and Campbell to exert a great influence in the future on the choice of animals studied by comparative psychologists.

Criticisms of Particular Psychological Work

Hodos and Campbell illustrate their criticisms by noting that Bitterman, in his studies of the "evolution of intelligence," compares teleost fish, turtles, pigeons, rats, and monkeys on learning tasks. These animals do not form an evolutionary sequence. No rat was ever an ancestor of a monkey; furthermore, it is not clear whether the rat and the monkey evolved their "ratlike" behavior characteristics (to use Bitterman's terminology) independently (convergence) or inherited the characteristics from some common reptilian ancestor (homology). Similarly, Harlow's examination of evolutionary trends in learning set performance lumps the New World monkeys with the Old World monkeys. Though these two groups probably had a common ancestor, their long isolation allowed evolution into quite different animals.

Behaviorial Evolutionary Studies

Hodos (1970) asks whether in fact studies of animals that are alive today tell us anything about ancestral animals. He has tried to show that the answer may be yes.

1. *A neuroanatomical example.* Hodos notes that textbooks commonly present the brains of representatives of various vertebrates, for example, codfish, frog, alligator, cat, and man (Truex and Carpenter 1964). These examples do not represent an evolutionary sequence. Given suitable assumptions and allowances for the nonavailability of ancestral animals, Hodos notes that the frog-alligator-goose comparison could represent stages in the evolution of bird brains, and a frog-alligator-cat comparison could represent stages in the evolution of carnivore brains.

2. *A behavioral example.* Hodos used data on learning sets in animals to illustrate a behavioral analysis. Learning sets were chosen because there has been a good deal of consistency in the methods of testing and presentation of data in the various studies. Hodos limited his search by looking only at the dependent measure of success of the animal on trial two of each successive problem. A high proportion of correct second-trial choices in a series of problems indicates that the animal has learned to learn, that is, it has acquired the principle; "correct on trial one, stay with that stimulus; incorrect on trial one, switch to another stimulus." In addition, Hodos presented data only from mature animals, to rule out ontogenic effects. (He was unable to obtain data for adult humans, so he relaxed his criteria to include data from human children.)

The performance of animals (that is, the percentage of

correct responses on trial two) after 100 problems for a variety of species is shown in Figure 13.1.

The only stem animal (that is, a living creature relatively similar to an ancestral animal) for which data were available was the tree shrew, an insectivore. This animal did not show evidence of learning to learn. However, in spite of the incomplete data, some conclusions are possible. Hodos noted that animals that are closely related (from an evolutionary point of view) acquire learning sets at similar rates. For example, the New World monkeys (Ceboidea) acquire the set at a low rate, the Old World monkeys (Cercopithecoidea) acquire the set at intermediate rates, and the great apes and humans (Hominoidea) acquire the set at the highest rate.

Arrangement of the available data in this form indicates the information that is urgently needed. The crucial animals appear to be the prosimians, marsupials, and reptiles. It is to be hoped that soon psychologists will turn to the study of these animals and fill the gap in the figure.

Hodos noted several problems in attributing behavioral differences in learning set to phylogenetic development:

1. The problem of reward. Most of the experiments reviewed used deprivation to motivate the animals in the task. We have no way of knowing whether the rats were as hungry as the ferrets, for example.

2. The problem of rearing. The animals used in different studies were raised in different settings, zoos, laboratories, and the wild. This may affect their performance.

3. The problem of sensory ability. All of the studies used visual stimuli for the problems. The relatively poor vision of the rat, for example, may have contributed to its poor performance. The use of olfactory stimuli might have produced a better performance from the rat.

4. The problem of the experimenter. The testing situation in all these studies is designed by humans and as such may be biased to demonstrate greater ability in humans. Were the

FIGURE 13.1

The learning set performance of different chordates. The numbers shown represent the percentage of correct choices in trial two of the 100th problem. From Hodos 1970, p. 36.

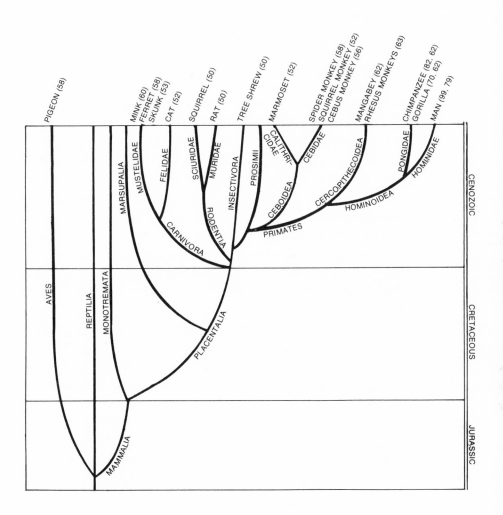

testing situations designed to reflect the animal's normal interaction with its natural environment? Probably not.

Hodos feels that these problems could lead to underestimating the ability of an animal at a task. If we correctly estimate its ability, as determined by a variety of studies, we may be approximating the animal's actual ability.

Analysis of Adaptations

Hodos and Campbell (1969) point out that not all comparative psychologists need to devote themselves to a study of the evolution of behavior. There are other issues. The analysis of adaptation, or differing degrees of development of some particular characteristic, is of interest. We can study the general relationships between the development of particular structures and their function in behavior.

We might also add that it would be interesting to study different abilities in a variety of species and then examine whether these abilities are related or whether they can be ordered sequentially in terms of their frequency among different species.

These tasks, together with the job of describing the behavioral capacities of each animal in the animal kingdom and determining whether there are systematic trends which perhaps might be correlated with other taxonomic indices, are legitimate goals for the comparative psychologist. Hodos and Campbell were not criticizing the goals, but the methodology of studies which have sought in the past to investigate the evolutionary development of particular behaviors.

A Behavioral or a Zoological Taxonomy?

King and Nichols (1960) note that the original objective of comparative psychology was to trace the evolution of behavior; the route taken toward this goal by comparative psychologists was the unqualified adoption of the zoological taxonomy of animals. They argue, however, that zoological taxonomy is inappropriate for investigating the evolution of behavior and that it remains inappropriate for comparative psychology even though goals have changed. The following reasons were given for this contention:

1. The zoological taxonomy is not a model that enables the psychologist to predict the behavior of one animal from that of another.*

2. The zoological taxonomy necessitates inferences based on extinct forms whose behavior cannot be studied.

3. Zoological taxonomy is often based on morphological structures which have little effect on behavior.†

King and Nichols feel that the development of a psychological taxonomy is needed. Although there is none yet, they suggest some possible directions a search should follow. They see comparative psychology as the study of the correlations between structure and function. (Notice how each psychologist has a different view of his discipline's goals.)

First, behavior must be defined. What is to be included? Motor movements, glandular secretions, nerve cell activity? Although some psychologists would object to each, all are probably needed for a complete behavioral analysis. The second problem is to devise a classification system. King and Nichols give examples of two kinds of classification systems— macroscopic and microscopic. A typical macroscopic system is derived from Nissen (1951):

---

* I do not agree with this particular point. In the previous chapter, where we reviewed the views of Hodos, I presented data on the ability of different animals in "learning to learn" (that is, in forming learning sets). It is clear from the data presented that animals that are taxonomically close are similar in their ability to learn how to learn.
† Hodos, as we have noted, felt that there is a useful correlation between morphology and behavior.

1. Anatomic-physiological foundations
   a. Differentiation of part and specialization of function
   b. Autonomy of parts and regenerative capacity or substitution of parts
   c. Poikilothermic versus homeothermic
   d. Maturation rate
2. Cognitive functions
   a. Sensory discriminations
   b. Perception
   c. Learning
   d. Abstraction, generalization, transfer, transposition
   e. Concepts and symbolic behavior
   f. Language
3. Motivational aspects
   a. Genetic and environmental determinism
   b. Biogenic versus psychogenic motivation
   c. Purpose
   d. Scope of needs
4. General adaptive characteristics
   a. Diversity, richness, and complexity of behavior
   b. Plasticity versus fixity of behavior
   c. Socialization, cooperation, specialization, and division of labor
   d. Cultural accretions
   e. Awareness and consciousness
   f. Behavior aberrations
   g. Importance of individual as opposed to race

A typical microscopic system is one described by Tinbergen (1951, p. 104) in dealing with the behavior of fish:

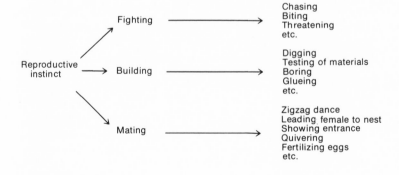

The question here is whether such schemes have any general usefulness, or whether they can be used only in narrow areas of interest.

It is always easy to criticize, but harder to suggest alternatives. The examples of psychological classification schemes discussed by King and Nichols have some uses, but in no way are they alternatives to the zoological taxonomy, and it is not clear how variants of these schemes could serve such a purpose. If I may be so bold as to suggest what King and Nichols ought to be saying—we need a zoological taxonomy that is based more on behavioral characteristics than on morphological, physiological, geographical, or paleontological traits.* If we had a taxonomy that placed greater stress on behavior, we could rate animals for the similarity of their behavior. This is what Bitterman has done in his comparative analysis of learning, in which he identified two kinds of behavior in certain tasks, fishlike and ratlike (though some have objected to his particular terminology). It would be interesting to compare zoological taxonomies based on different sources of data—behavior, anatomy, geography, and so on. Where would the coincidences be and where would the differences arise?

It is clear that our knowledge of different capacities and abilities in different species is not yet adequate for the task of looking for behavioral similarities and differences between species. In time, as data accumulate, this will become possible. It took many hundreds of years to develop an adequate zoological taxonomy. We should consider ourselves lucky if it takes only another 50 years to develop an alternative taxonomy based on behavior.

---

*Of course, zoological taxonomy sometimes does use behavior as a basis for deciding on the taxonomic position of particular species, as for example in classifying birds related to pigeons through their manner of drinking. However, what I am suggesting here is a greater reliance on behavioral traits.

Comparative Psychology: Does It Exist?

It may seem absurd to ask whether comparative psychology exists, yet Lockard (1971), in a recent article entitled "Reflections on the fall of comparative psychology," states: "What we once knew as comparative psychology has been overrun by a scientific revolution. In the wake of that revolution lies the debris of what was once a traditional branch of psychology, now a confused scatter of views of nature, problems, and methods" (p. 168). Let us examine his evidence for such a statement.

Evidence for a Fall

Lockard argues that comparative psychology in the 1950s worked itself into an untenable position. It restricted work on animals to the study of a few species (primarily the white rat [Beach 1950]) and it accepted a set of untenable premises about animal behavior. Let me quickly summarize and respond to Lockard's view of these untenable premises:

"Untenable premise" 1. There is a phylogenetic scale, a linear arrangement from simple to complex, unintelligent to intelligent, protozoa to man. Lockard says it is difficult to argue for the existence of a phylogenetic scale. As Hodos and Campbell (1969) have pointed out, using current species, it is difficult, if not impossible, to trace the evolution of a particular behavior, since the ancestral species through which the behavior evolved are no longer available for study. This is true. Though there may be no *phylogenetic* scale, however, there could well be a *phyletic* scale. A phyletic scale implies no assumptions as to how the behavior evolved. Rather, it says that different species may be ordered along some dimension in such a way that even changes in one's criteria result in the same order each time. For example, Heffner and Masterton (1970) compared the auditory capacities of several species of mammals and concluded that some of the variables studies

170

showed linear progressions when the species were arranged according to the phyletic scale. For example, the species showed an increase in their sensitivity at 1kHz from possum to hedgehog to tree shrew to prosimian to macaque to chimpanzee to man. The same linear sequence was also found for the variables of high frequency cut-off and lowest threshold, while for two other variables there was no linear trend (best frequency and area of audible field). It may be reasonable for Lockard to assert that there is no phylogenetic scale, but to state that animals cannot be ordered on some scale (whether taxonomic distance or merely an ordering based on the examination of some other variable such as auditory sensitivity) is patently incorrect.

"Untenable premise" 2. The comparative method is essentially a scaling problem of arranging animals of different degrees of intelligence on the phylogenetic scale. Lockard notes that many psychologists have focused on the problem of comparing species for their "degree of intelligence" and that such a problem has little meaning. The behaviors investigated as indications of intelligence involved a number of abilities and were most likely related to variables such as the ecological demands on the animal. Even if we grant Lockard's argument here, the errors of past psychologists do not invalidate the discipline. That psychologists used to debate whether all completed suicides were insane or not, a question which is now considered meaningless (that is, unanswerable), does not herald the "fall" either of abnormal psychology or of suicidology (Lester 1971). It indicates what we would judge to be desirable, namely, that as knowledge accumulates, the discipline moves on. That we no longer ask the same questions in comparative psychology that were asked 20 years ago is a relief. It means comparative psychology has progressed.

Let us hurry over the rest of Lockard's list of premises:

(3) Animals lower in the phylogenetic scale are simpler than man but not fundamentally different, and (4) most animals

171

are pretty much alike. (5) Learning is the key to animal behavior because most behavior is acquired, and (6) genetics and evolution are irrelevant to animal behavior. (7) There are laws of behavior best formulated in paradigms based on experimental research, and (8) animal behavior can best be studied in the laboratory because of the controlled conditions. (9) The best variables to study are physical ones.

"Premises" 3-9 are gross generalizations that do not apply to many of the studies that were conducted under the discipline of comparative psychology. It is well known that a good way to argue is to set up straw men and then knock them down; since straw men can have defects tailored into them, they are easier to criticize than reality.

True, there were some psychologists who argued for the preeminence of learning in the development of behavior. But there were others who argued for the influence of innate factors. The Gestalt psychologists (with a nativist tradition, assuming that most perceptual capacities are innate) encouraged studies that looked for and found evidence for the perceptual constancies in lower animals, such as chickens, fish, and dogs. There *were* some psychologists who preferred to study animal behavior in the laboratory, but there were also psychologists like Schneirla who studied animal behavior in the field. It is noteworthy that Schneirla teamed up with Maier (a psychologist who worked in the laboratory) to write perhaps the classic text on comparative psychology, one that is still in print (Maier and Schneirla 1964).

There are perhaps three main points to make in response to Lockard's premises 3-9: (1) the existence of errors in the past does not invalidate a discipline; (2) not all psychologists held those premises; (3) the abandonment of past beliefs does not necessarily invalidate a discipline. Einstein's innovations and modifications of the laws of classical physics did not lead to the "fall" of physics (or even, for that matter, classical physics).

Behavioral Biology

What did Lockard propose as the wave of the future, the replacement for comparative psychology? According to him, it is behavioral biology that has won out over comparative psychology. The essence of this discipline is "ethology," linked up with genetics, ecology, developmental biology, and physiological ecology. Lockard believes that two important principles guide behavioral biology: (1) phylogenetic relatedness—behavioral homologies increase in frequency and detail among different animal species as proximity to a common ancestral species increases, and (2) similar behaviors among unrelated species result from similar selection pressures.

Lockard did not dwell on modern behavioral biology in detail, so perhaps there is no need for us to dwell long on it here. Two points are worth making, however. First, some of the workers in behavioral biology make statements as extreme and as naive as those by old comparative psychologists, which Lockard criticized. Lorenz (1966), whom Lockard acknowledges as one of those who gave behavioral biology its impetus, has proposed such premises as (1) genetics and evolution are the key to animal behavior because so little animal behavior is learned, (2) most animals are pretty much alike (and it is quite in order to generalize from infrahuman species to man), and (3) animals can best be studied in the field. These premises, when compared with those listed by Lockard as being held by the old comparative psychologists, are equally extreme and in no way herald the fall of behavioral biology.

Second, we may note that the first principle proposed by Lockard, as underlying the new behavioral biology, seems pretty much like the old premise of the existence of a phylogenetic scale. Animals *can* be described according to their phylogenetic relatedness, it seems. Obviously such a statement is not as crude as the premise of a simple phylogenetic scale, but then it is 1970 and not 1950, and science does progress.

173

Whither Comparative Psychology?

Let us leave criticism of Lockard's thesis and move on to a more fruitful area, namely, where is comparative psychology going? It is relatively easy to identify some potentially rewarding and exciting areas of research that are beginning to emerge in comparative psychology. Perhaps the detailing of some of these trends may help researchers to build on them.

There are those who believe, with some justification, that the describing of the phenomenon must precede the derivation of laws about the phenomenon. It must be admitted, however, that such a strategy does not appeal to all. In the past, behaviors of many species have been described and the processes underlying them examined. There have appeared several good compendia of facts about animal behavior (for example, Marler and Hamilton 1966). But the term *comparative psychology* suggests the comparison of one species with another rather than the isolated study of each species.

1. Accordingly, one early trend in comparative psychology was the simultaneous study of several species. Rather than placing members of one species on a visual cliff, members of several species can be tested (Schiffman 1970). Similarly, it may be asked which species show response alternation and from which phyla these species come (Lester 1968). The work by Heffner and Masterton (1970) mentioned above is a good example of this. They ordered their data on the hearing abilities of several mammalian species along a dimension of "recency of common ancestry to man." They could as easily have used a dimension such as taxonomic relatedness (or even, for that matter, a concept called the phyletic scale, proposed illogically years ago, but which still seems to order the animal species in a plausible way). They found certain hearing abilities linearly related to this dimension. For those who might object to the use of this dimension, it is easily possible to modify the presentation of data. A variable such as sensitivity to 1kHz can be taken as the primary dimension and the remaining variables

plotted against it. Or better still, the variables can be intercorrelated throughout species, and those which are related can be identified.

2. The latter suggestion has been carried out in some studies. For example, Twyver (1969) examined electroencephalographic recordings for five rodent species (hamster, rat, mouse, ground squirrel, and chinchilla). He found species differences in the amount of sleep each day and in the proportion of paradoxical sleep.*

Twyver is representative of the new comparative psychologist, however, in that he took a second variable and correlated it with these EEG measures. He compared hibernators with nonhibernators and found that hibernators slept in significantly longer periods, had higher percentages of paradoxical sleep and slightly higher percentages of total sleep time. They also appeared to sleep more deeply.

3. To further illustrate this kind of approach, a study by King et al. (1967) can provide data. They studied the climbing, running, gnawing, swimming, and digging behavior of eight species of deer mice (*Peromyscus*) and found no association between the performance measures at these tasks and either taxonomic relatedness or ecological differences in their natural habitats.

However, if we correlate performance measures for the eight species (see Table 13.1), we get the results of a *cross-species study,* from which we might conclude that climbing and running ability are not related in species of Peromyscus, while the behaviors of gnawing and running are related.

This kind of analysis has not appeared frequently in comparative psychology, yet it is quite common in anthropology under the name of cross-cultural studies. A number of cultures, nonliterate societies, for example (Lester 1967), or literate societies (Rudin 1968), are taken, and two or more variables

---

*Deep behavioral sleep accompanied by electrical activity in the brain, which is characteristic of behavioral alertness.

are correlated for the sample of cultures. This method has been used to test many hypotheses derived from theories of personality (for example, Whiting and Child 1954).

The possibility of cross-species studies conducted analogously holds great promise for comparative psychology. Hypotheses may be testable by selecting a sample of animal species and then correlating behavioral (or biological) variables (or both) over the species. The species may be chosen from across phyla or within phyla. The results may differ considerably, depending on the range of species sampled. For example, phyletic trends in social behavior are easily identified, while trends within, say, the primates are not (Scott 1969), for the latter differences may be too complex and subtle for us to measure, given the present state of the art.

If comparative psychology has fallen, perhaps we can take heart from the fact that many falls occur before one can be proud.

TABLE 13.1

The intercorrelations of five performance measures over eight species of Peromyscus. Data from King et al. (1967) and rank order correlations computed by Lester.

	running	climbing	digging	gnawing
swimming	+0.19	−0.27	+0.36	−0.26
running		0.00	−0.69	−0.76
climbing			−0.52	+0.07
digging				+0.59

References

Beach, F.A. 1950. The snark was a boojum. *American Psychologist* 5:115-24.

Bernard, L. L. 1924. *Instinct*. New York: Holt.

Boice, R. 1970. Avoidance learning in active and passive frogs and toads. *Journal of Comparative and Physiological Psychology* 70:154-56.

Brower, L. P.; and Brower, J. V. Z. 1962. Investigations into mimicry. *Natural History* 71(4):8-19.

Cofer, C. N.; and Appley, M. H. 1964. *Motivation*. New York: Wiley.

Hebb, D. O. 1953. Heredity and environment in mammalian behavior. *British Journal of Animal Behavior* 1:43-47.

Heffner, H.; and Masterton, B. 1970. Hearing in primitive primates. *Journal of Comparative and Physiological Psychology* 71:175-82.

Hodos, W. 1970. Evolutionary interpretation of neural and behavioral studies of living vertebrates. In *The neurosciences: second study program,* ed. F. O. Schmitt, pp. 26-39. New York: Rockefeller Press.

Hodos, W.; and Campbell, C.B.G. 1969. Scala naturae. *Psychological Review* 76:337-50.

King, J.; and Nichols, J. W. 1960. Problems of classification. In *Principles of comparative psychology,* ed. R. H. Waters, D. A. Rethlingshafer, and W. E. Caldwell, pp. 18-42. New York: McGraw-Hill.

King, J.; Price, E.; and Weber. P. 1967. Behavioral comparisons within the genus Peromyscus. *Papers of the Michigan Academy of Science, Arts, and Letters* 53:113-36.

Lehrman, D. S. 1953. A critique of Konrad Lorenz's theory of instinctive behavior. *Quarterly Review of Biology* 28:337-36.

Lester, D. 1967. Suicide, homicide, and the effects of socialization. *Journal of Personality and Social Psychology* 5:466-68.

———. 1968. Response alternation. *Journal of Psychology* 69: 131-42.

———. 1971. Relationship of mental disorder to suicidal behavior. *New York State Medical Journal* 71:1,503-1,505.

Lockard, R. B. 1971. Reflections on the fall of comparative psychology. *American Psychologist* 26:168-79.

Lorenz, K. 1966. *On aggression.* New York: Harcourt.

Maier, N.; and Schneirla, T. C. 1964. *Principles of animal psychology.* New York: Dover.

Marler, P.; and Hamilton, W. D. 1966. *Mechanisms of animal behavior.* New York: Wiley.

Nissen, H. W. 1951. Phylogenetic comparison. In *Handbook of experimental psychology,* ed. S. S. Stevens, pp. 347-86. New York: Wiley.

Rudin, S. 1968. National motives predict psychogenic death rates. *Science* 160:901-903.

177

Schiffman, H. R. 1970. Evidence for sensory dominance. *Journal of Comparative and Physiological Psychology* 71:38-41.

Scott, J. P. 1969. The social psychology of infrahuman animals. In *The handbook of social psychology,* vol. 1, ed. G. Lindzey and E. Aronson, pp. 611-42. Reading, Mass.: Addison-Wesley.

————. 1970. Biology and human aggression. *American Journal of Orthopsychiatry* 40:568-76.

Tinbergen, N. 1951. *The study of instinct.* London: Oxford Univ. Press.

Truex, R. C.; and Carpenter, M. B. 1964. *Strong and Elwyn's Human Neuroanatomy.* Baltimore: Williams and Wilkins.

Twyver, H. V. 1969. Sleep patterns of five rodent species. *Physiology and Behavior* 4:901-905.

Watson, J. B. 1924. *Behaviorism.* New York: Norton.

Willems, E. P.; and Raush, H. L., eds. 1969. *Naturalist viewpoints in psychological research.* New York: Holt, Rinehart & Winston.

Whiting, J.; and Child, I. 1954. *Child training and personality.* New Haven: Yale Univ. Press.

Chapter 14

Comparative Psychology and Man

STUDENTS OFTEN ASK why psychologists spend time studying animals. How does knowing about animals help us to understand man? they ask. In the introduction to this book, I pointed out that the aim of psychology is the *study of behavior*—not just human behavior, but all behavior. Thus the study of behavior in animals other than man is of interest in and of itself. In addition, as I have frequently pointed out, the psychologist is also interested in phyletic trends in behavior. How does the mechanism responsible for a particular behavior or set of behaviors change as one moves from lower to higher species? How do the behaviors themselves change? For example, if we could identify phylogenetic and ontogenetic trends (changes in behavior as an organism develops from infant to adult), we could test, in the behavioral sphere, the embryological motto, "ontogeny recapitulates phylogeny." In this way, too, the study of animals can give information about man's behavior. In addition, man may benefit by studying animal behavior, which would also help him put subhumans to better use. In this chapter we will review some of the ways in which the study of animals aids man.

The Use of Animals in the Labor Force

Much of the activity men engage in is boring, monotonous, even degrading. Fruit-picking, garbage-collection, house-painting, and assembly line work are examples. Bernstein and Alloway (1969) have suggested that such activities could and should be carried out by alternative organisms.

There are numerous examples in our history of the use of animals to aid man in his labor. Dogs have been used to herd sheep, guard property, and lead the blind; horses have been used as beasts of burden and as a means of transportation, and so on.

In recent times psychologists have investigated how animals can be used for considerably more delicate tasks. Skinner (1960) showed how pigeons could be used to guide missiles into targets, and Cumming (1966) trained pigeons to inspect diodes for paint defects. In these studies the spontaneous behavioral repertoires of the animals are utilized, but they are deflected to some new purpose. Other work has been done involving much more drastic modifications in the organisms' behaviors. Bernstein and Alloway related a report from South Africa which described how baboons were being trained to drive tractors and used to plant and harvest crops. (One wonders whether South Africa will someday find itself with the problems of a multispecific,* as well as a multiracial, society.) Bernstein and Alloway suggest that subhumans could be used extensively to replace man in menial tasks. Primates could be used to pick fruit, collect garbage, and so on. Pigeons could be used for quality control. Perhaps porpoises could be trained to act as lifeguards at beaches, primates as mailmen, and pigeons as radar screen scanners. The possibilities are enormous.

The use of other organisms for these tasks can enable man to turn to tasks more fitting to him—to do that which he alone is capable of. There may be emotional objections

* Made up of many species.

to these ideas, especially from those who are concerned about cruelty to animals. However, cruelty to humans is an equally important principle.

Clearly, the knowledge amassed by the comparative psychologist is going to be essential if these ideas are ever to become a reality. The training of animals and the decisions on which animals will be suited to which tasks will require detailed knowledge about the different organisms under consideration.

The Use of Animals to Aid in Understanding Man

There are many important experiments that cannot be carried out on man, for ethical reasons. It is not possible to carry out experimental brain surgery on humans in order to investigate the functions of particular parts of the central nervous system. It is not possible to inject newly discovered chemicals in order to see what the effects on behavior will be. It is not ethical to stress man to such an extent that permanent physical or psychological damage will result.

Yet some of these studies are crucial if we are to understand how the central nervous system operates, if we are to develop new drugs for the treatment of diseases, and if we are to understand and control behavior.

Furthermore, it may well be that some of the mechanisms underlying the behavior of man are identical to those underlying similar behaviors in other animals. Therefore we can discover these mechanisms by studying animals rather than man.

There are some psychologists who maintain that man is so different from other animals that nothing of value to the understanding of man's behavior can be learned from the study of the other animals (Mehlman 1967, for example). Such an extreme position is foolish. To be sure, there are differences between man and other animals, but just as surely there are similarities. Where there are similarities, we can learn about man from a direct study of other animals. Even where there

181

are differences, we can test our techniques, concepts, and tools by working with simpler organisms before we turn to the complex phenomenon of man.

To illustrate how comparative psychology can have interesting implications for man, we will consider two examples: Richter on the welfare state and Skinner on teaching.

The Comparative Psychologist Turns to Man: Rats, Man, and the "Welfare State"

Richter (1959) has worked for many years with the rat and has frequently compared domesticated, laboratory-bred rats with captured, wild rats. The Norway rat arrived in Europe about 1730 and in America about 1790. Somewhere between 1840 and 1850 captured Norwegian rats were brought into the laboratory and bred for use in experiments. Since then the rat has been used extensively in research of all kinds. This gives us an opportunity to study what happens to an animal when it moves from a wild state, in which it has to struggle to exist, to a protected state, where all of its needs are provided for by someone else.

Richter has summarized the changes that occurred in the rat as a result of domestication and protection: (1) the adrenal glands, which are involved in reactions to stress and fatigue and in providing protection from several diseases, have become smaller and less effective in the laboratory rat; (2) the thyroid gland, which helps to regulate metabolism, has become less active; (3) the gonads develop earlier, function more regularly, and thus bring about greater fertility; (4) the brain has become smaller and the central nervous system is more susceptible to audiogenic and other types of seizures.

Why has this happened? Richter argues that in the wild, only the strongest, fittest, most active rats survive. In contrast, in the laboratory, which is a highly protective environment, weak and puny individuals may survive. They do not have to fend for themselves, but are provided for. In addition, mutations that have developed have survived because of the protective environment, whereas in the wild they might have been eliminated in the struggle for survival.

Early in man's history an individual had to be fit, active, healthy, and resourceful in order to survive. But as more and more protection became available, first by legislation and then by medicine, less and less health and intelligence were necessary for survival. Richter points out that today unhealthy individuals survive and are able to reproduce, and so add to the population of unhealthy individuals. Jennings (1927), a biologist and a humanitarian, has written:

> Defects in genes become as open to remedy as defects in nutrition. A defective thyroid product is replaced by manufactured thyroxin, the individual is restored to normality. But his genes are not changed; they remain defective; they are transmitted to his descendants. His descendants too must be treated with thyroxin. . . . In time the race thus accumulates a great stock of these defective genes. Each individual that receives them must be treated with one or more of the substitutes for the normal products of the genes. Each must carry with him an arsenal of hypodermic syringes, of vials, of capsules, of tablets. (pp. 46-47)

Richter himself tried to document how the incidence of individuals with physical and mental defects has increased with the development of modern culture and technology, how the incidence of neoplastic diseases (that is, cancer) has increased, how the incidence of circulatory diseases, mental diseases, diabetes, and hypersensitive diseases have increased. Man, like the laboratory rat, is becoming less fit, less healthy, less able to fend for himself.

What do we do? Simply put, Richter argues that knowledge is important. If we are aware of what is happening, we can perhaps plan for it, control it, and understand it. He doesn't argue for a return to a more primitive life, though this, too, is a solution.

We have discussed Richter's ideas in order to illustrate how the comparative psychologist can use his knowledge of one species to make generalizations about another, in this case man. Of course, Richter's ideas are speculative, but they are a warning, one, perhaps, we should note.

The Comparative Psychologist Turns to Man: Teaching Machines

Skinner has oriented his studies on learning around the belief that contemporary research should focus primarily on the collection of data and accumulation of knowledge, rather than on the construction of theories. He suggests that behavioral scientists should concentrate on learning how organisms respond to particular stimuli. Skinner himself narrowed his interest to the study of operant conditioning, in which emitted responses can be made more or less likely by the appropriate use of reinforcement.

As one part of his investigations, Skinner designed a situation for investigating learning in which the organism is placed in a small, barren chamber. For a rat, this chamber may possess one bar which is capable of being depressed, a panel on which stimuli may be displayed, and a cup in which pellets of food may be placed.

One of the animals studied most by Skinner has been the pigeon. Many aspects of his work with pigeons are relevant to education, but here we will consider the concept of shaping. Let us see how a pigeon can be trained to turn clockwise in a continuous swift movement. If we waited until this response occurred spontaneously and then rewarded the animal, so that this response would be learned by a trial and error method, we probably would wait a long time. Using shaping, we can produce the response in a couple of minutes. First, the experimenter reinforces any response that contributes to clockwise movement. For example, when the pigeon turns his head to the right, we can drop a pellet of food into the cup. (Obviously, for the learning to proceed quickly, the pigeon must be habituated to the apparatus, have experience in feeding at the cup, and be hungry.) After the pigeon has eaten the food, similar movements can be reinforced for a period of time. Then the reinforcement is witheld until a response is made that is more of a clockwise turn, for example, a head turn plus the left foot stepping forward. This process is repeated, each time demanding a closer approximation to the required response before food reinforcement is given. Within a short time the pigeon will be making a clockwise turn.

A pigeon can be reinforced for responding when certain stimuli are present but not reinforced in the presence of other stimuli. In this way discrimination of color, brightness, shape, and so on can be studied.

Work with a large number of animals leads to two necessities: instrumentation and eventually computer management. Otherwise, one human is needed for every animal being conditioned, and humans make more recording errors than machines do. Working out machine control of the conditioning forces led Skinner to wonder whether human education might be more adequately managed by machines (Skinner 1961).

A teaching machine will work best in shaping appropriate behavior if it uses particular methods. First, the student should compose his own response rather than select it from alternatives. Not only will this facilitate recall (rather than mere recognition), but presenting him with incorrect responses in a multiple-choice format might mean he would learn the incorrect responses rather than the correct one. Second, the student must be led through a carefully graded sequence of steps that increase in complexity and move toward the final stage of the behavior we wish him to learn. Third, the student must be given immediate feedback on his performance. After each response the student must be informed whether his response is correct or not.

In a modern teaching machine this can be arranged by using a teletype outlet to a central computer, with a visual or typed display unit. The student makes his responses by typing some phrase on the teletype, and the display gives feedback to the student and displays the next step in the pre-programmed sequence.

A teaching machine possesses several advantages over classroom teaching. There is a constant rather than intermittent exchange between teacher and student. The structure of the situation insures that the student masters less complex material before moving on to more complex material. The student is presented with material which he is prepared for and competent to tackle. The student is reinforced for every correct response. Finally, each student can proceed at his own pace with the material. In some ways, therefore, a teaching machine resembles a private tutor rather than the traditional classroom teacher.

Skinner has strongly advocated the power of appropriate reinforcement in shaping our lives and has suggested, in a novel called *Walden Two,* how judicious use of reinforcement could lead to a utopian existence (Skinner 1948).

References

Bernstein, D. A.; and Alloway, T. M. 1969. On the use of alternative organisms. *Journal of Applied Psychology* 53:506-509.

Cumming, W. W. 1966. A bird's eye glimpse of men and machines. In *The control of human behavior,* ed. R. Ulrich, T. Stachnik, and J. Mabry, pp. 246-56. Glenview, Ill.: Scott Foresman.

Jennings, H. S. 1927. Public health progress and race progress: are they incompatible? *Science* 66:45-50.

Mehlman, B. 1967. Animal research and human psychology. *Journal of Humanistic Psychology* 7:66-79.

Richter, C. P. 1959. Rats, man, and the welfare state. *American Psychologist* 14:18-28.

Skinner, B. F. 1948. *Walden two.* New York: Macmillan.

———. 1960. Pigeons in a pelican. *American Psychologist* 13:28-37.

———. 1961. Teaching machines. *Scientific American* 205(5): 90-102.

Chapter 15

Conclusion

I N SPITE OF the fact that there has been much criticism of comparative psychology, it is apparent that much progress has been made, and that some trends for the future of comparative psychology can be detected. First, let us briefly review the criticism.

Criticisms of Comparative Psychology

In the past, comparative psychologists have been criticized for using too few species in their research, often focusing on the white rat to the exclusion of other species (Beach 1950). This criticism is actually true only for noncomparative psychologists. It is true that the psychologist interested in learning theory or brain function has used the white rat extensively in the past. But, the comparative psychologist has always used a variety of species, and increasingly, all experimental psychologists are using a variety of species in their research. However, many species of animals do not take easily to laboratory conditions and cannot be subjected to the same standardized tasks as common laboratory animals. For example, prairie dogs cannot be subjected to the same deprivation conditions (deprivation of water and food) as rats in order to motivate them; they simply die of starvation.

This brings us to the second criticism of comparative psychology, reliance on laboratory experiments. In order to study quantitative differences between different species, it is necessary to test them in a standardized task. It was noted in Chapter 8 that Gossette (1968) has argued that spatial habit reversal tasks reveal quantitative rather than qualitative differences between species. On the other hand, Bitterman (1965) has argued for qualitative differences in the learning ability of different species. In this latter case, we could explore a variety of testing tasks (each specifically designed for the particular species) in order to see whether the animal can show the behavior being studied or not.

Because the task is often not suited to the animal, we can only conclude that the animal is *at least* as "intelligent" as our tests show. It may be capable of more than we can demonstrate—which was illustrated by the study that reported that toads can learn an avoidance task in one trial if the object to be avoided is an insect that stings (Brower and Brower 1962), but not if the task is one of avoiding electric shock in a box (Boice 1970).

We reviewed Hodos' and Campbell's criticism (1969) of the attempts by comparative psychologists to trace the evolution of behavior. The commonly studied sequence rat-cat-monkey does not provide such data, since the rat is not ancestral to the cat and the cat is not ancestral to the monkey. This criticism has been sidestepped in this book, in that I have not attempted to trace the evolution of behavior; instead, I have tried to see whether there are regular changes in behavior of different animal species as we move from simple animals such as the amoeba to complex animals such as man.

I have used the notion of a phyletic scale. In fact, the work of this book can be seen as an attempt to provide a rational basis for the existence of a phyletic scale. If we can detect regular changes or order the different species on the basis of performance in one or more tasks, then we have a basis for a proposed phyletic scale. Clearly, if Bitterman's work on learning is validated, "fishlike" behavior would be toward one end of the scale and "ratlike" behavior toward the other end.

Furthermore, although Hodos and Campbell criticized comparative psychologists, they point to the direction research could take if the aim were to trace the evolution of behavior. They gave the sequence frog-alligator-goose and frog-alligator-cat as two possible approximations of evolutionary paths.

Phyletic Trends

Leaving this criticism and the rebuttals to them, we might ask whether phyletic differences and trends have been noted. It is clear from the body of this book that there are many phyletic trends that have been noted in all areas of psychology —in social behavior, learning, perceptual abilities, and so on.

Furthermore, it is interesting to note that the literature of psychology is full of statements that involve phyletic differences and trends, which are often not documented with empirical support or explored for their full implications.

At the microscopic level we can point to statements such as that of Scott (1969), that a mouse will die if allowed to eat only every 24 hours, whereas a dog will not; or that deprived rats drink first, whereas deprived guinea pigs eat first. Schiffman (1970) placed young animals of different species on the glass over the deep and the shallow sides of a visual cliff and noted their responses. He found that hamsters, mice, and gerbils were haptically (touch) oriented and if placed over the deep side on the glass were indifferent to visual cues. On the other hand, other animals seemed to be visually oriented: pigmented rabbits moved away from the deep side toward the shallow side when placed on the glass; albino rabbits and guinea pigs trembled when placed on the glass over the deep side but did not move, and kittens mewed more but did not move. Finally, to give a morphological example, Ficken et al. (1971) noted that birds with eye markings (lines leading forward from the eyes) feed on swiftly moving prey; Ficken suggests that these lines may serve to help the animal "aim" for the prey.

At the macroscopic level there are many phyletic trends that have been proposed (again, often without substantial empirical or quantitative support). For example, Denny and Ratner (1970) noted phyletic trends in consummatory behavior: (1) the number and variety of stimuli to which consummatory behavior is directed seems to increase with phyletic level, (2) there is a greater diversity of stimuli for consummatory behavior for higher animals—that is, there are more ways of satisfying a need (as in the sexual deviations found in the highest animals), and (3) behavior is more plastic, that is, many different stimuli can elicit the same consummatory response, there is a greater incentive value of novel stimuli, novel stimuli are incentives for the consummatory responses of contacting and manipulating, and the same stimuli can elicit many responses.

Another example here is the contention of Lorenz (1966) that the animals with more "intelligent" behavior tend to have longer periods during which they are dependent on their parents.

Interestingly, such statements abound in psychology, with little empirical data to support them, but psychology is a science in which statistics are ubiquitous. No one has ever tried to compute the exact correlation between the time for which the young of a species are dependent on their parents and the learning ability of the adult members of the species, yet in few other areas of psychology would such statements go untested or unchallenged.

The Future of Comparative Psychology

The future of comparative psychology is perhaps more interesting that the past, because it is in the future that the exciting work will come. There are many possibilities for future research. First, it may soon be possible to order the different animal species on a dimension with an empirical rationale. For example, if we take operant conditioning, it may be possible to assign numbers to different species to indicate their abilities on some particular task. We will then have a rational phyletic scale. Second, we may soon be able to carry out cross-species studies, much as psychologists and other social scientists now carry out cross-cultural studies. Is the learning ability of different animals related to their emotionality? It is difficult to test this hypothesis in rats, for example, for years of inbreeding have reduced the individual variability of the members of the species. Furthermore, a test of the hypothesis with rats might have limited generality. We could, however, take a sample of animal species and explore the strength of such an association, if there is one. (A previous warning should be reiterated here—that the range of species from which the animals are taken may affect the conclusions. We have noted that trends in social behavior, for example, are clearer *between* phyla than *within* phyla.)

A third possibility is that we may be able to create a Guttman scale (Edwards 1957) of behaviors. That is, if an animal shows behavior *n,* then we know it will show behaviors 1, 2, ... , (*n*-1). For example, according to data presented by Scott (1969), we can conclude that if the members of a phylum show epimeletic behavior, they will also show sexual behavior, and if they show sexual behavior, they will also show ingestive behavior, whereas the converse of these statements is not true. A Guttman scale of behaviors might also provide a rationale for the phyletic ordering of animals.

It may be predicted, therefore, that comparative psychology will accumulate basic data rapidly in the future and that general laws will soon be identifiable and testable. Comparative psychology at the moment is in a kind of adolescence, but it is clearly moving toward adulthood.

References

Beach, F. A. 1950. The snark was a boojum. *American Psychologist* 5:115-24.

Bitterman, M. E. 1965. Phyletic differences in learning. *American Psychologist* 20:217-27.

Boice, R. 1970. Avoidance learning in active and passive frogs and toads. *Journal of Comparative and Physiological Psychology* 70:154-56.

Brower, L. P.; and Brower, J. V. Z. 1962. Investigations into mimicry. *Natural History* 71(4):8-19.

Denny, M. R.; and Ratner, S. C. 1970. *Comparative psychology.* Homewood, Ill.: Dorsey.

Edwards, A. L. 1957. *Techniques of attitude scale construction.* New York: Appleton-Century-Crofts.

Ficken, R. W.; Matthiae, P. E.; and Horwich, R. 1971. Eye marks in vertebrates. *Science* 173:936-39.

Gossette, R. L. 1968. Examination of retention decrement explanation of comparative successive discrimination reversal learning by birds and mammals. *Perceptual and Motor Skills* 27:1,147-52.

Hodos, W.; and Campbell, C. B. G. 1969. Scala naturae. *Psychological Review* 76:337-50.

Lorenz, K. 1966. *On aggression.* New York: Harcourt Brace & World.

Schiffman, H. R. 1970. Evidence for sensory dominance. *Journal of Comparative and Physiological Psychology* 71:38-41.

Scott, J. P. 1969. The social psychology of infrahuman animals. In *The handbook of social psychology,* vol. 1, ed. G. Lindzey and E. Aronson, pp. 611-42. Reading, Mass.: Addison-Wesley.

Indexes

Animal Index

Animal Index

Animal Index

Proboscidea, 14
prosimians, 96, 124, 161, 164, 165, 171
Prototheria, 13
Protozoa, 7, 13, 38, 43, 55, 62, 63, 102, 103, 110, 120, 132, 170
Pseudomys elegans, 72
Pseudovespa vulgaris, 92

quail, 135

rabbit, 14, 51, 72, 80, 91, 189
raccoon, 106, 109
rat, 9, 14, 30, 50, 59, 61, 72, 76, 78, 80, 81, 86, 87, 88, 93, 105, 106, 108, 111, 122, 123, 125, 126, 136, 161, 162, 165, 175, 182, 184, 187, 188, 189, 191
Rana catesbeiana, 12
Rana pipiens, 75
reptile, 7, 13, 27, 51, 60, 72, 92, 124, 125, 141, 142, 164, 165
rhinoceros, 14
ribbon worm, 13
ringdove, 79
rodent, 7, 14, 51, 57, 72, 124, 140, 161, 165, 175
roundworm, 120

Sarcophaga, 82, 92
sea lily, 39
scallop, 65
Schistocerca gregaria, 76, 78, 83
sciuridae, 165
scorpion, 56
sea anemone, 110
sea cow, 14
sea cucumber, 39
sea squirt, 13
sea urchin, 39, 48, 120
Serranelus subligarius, 121
shark, 13, 27
sheep, 72, 88, 131, 134, 135, 142, 180
shrew, 14
Siamese fighting fish, 90
silkworm, 24, 64
silverfish, 43
Sipunculida, 13
Sirenia, 14
skunk, 109, 165
sloth, 14
snail, 10, 56, 65, 101, 120, 121

snake, 27, 57, 141
snow leopard, 72
Solenopsis, 57
sowbug, 123
spider, 30, 57, 92, 120
sponge, 13, 38, 120, 160
squid, 56, 92, 120
squirrel, 165
starfish, 38, 39, 65, 120
stick insect, 141
stickleback, 78
swallow, 110

tapeworm, 121
Tardigrada, 13
tarsier, 161
Tealia, 103
teleost fish, 59, 110, 162
Tenebrio molitor, 123
termite, 41, 92, 130
Terrapena carolina, 72
Theria, 13
tiger, 12, 72
toad, 158, 188
tree shrew, 164, 165, 171
Trichogaster trichopterus sumatranus, 126
trumpeter, 109
Tubulidentata, 14
turkey, 135
turtle, 27, 72, 106, 108, 162

Uca pugnax, 75
ungulate, 50, 57, 124, 140
Urochordata, 13

vertebrates, 7, 13, 56, 61, 62, 89, 91, 96, 104, 120, 125, 130
Vespidae, 49
Viverridae, 124
Vorticella nebulifera, 102
Vulpes pallida, 12

wasp, 49, 82, 92, 121
whale, 12, 14
wolf, 12, 131, 150, 158
worm, 10, 13, 55, 120, 121

Xiphophorus helleri, 50

Author Index

Author Index

Ellis, A., 127

Fellows, B.J., 84, 97
Ficken, R. W., 190, 192
Fleure, H. J., 103, 112
Fox, M. W., 139, 147, 148, 150, 152

Gardner, B. J., 151, 152
Gardner, R. A., 151, 152
Gibson, E. J., 69, 70, 71, 72, 73, 74, 78, 93, 97, 99
Gilbert, R. M., 28, 31, 112
Glickman, S. E., 70, 72, 73, 98, 124, 126, 139, 148
Goldstein, K., 143, 148
Gonzales, R. C., 109, 112
Gossette, R. L., 108, 113, 188, 192
Gould, J. L., 150, 152
Grainger, D., 127
Gray, P. H., 31
Greenhut, A. M., 76, 97
Gregory, R. L., 55, 58, 66

Hahn, E., 151, 152
Hamilton, C. R., 77, 97
Hamilton, W., 4, 8, 54, 61, 66, 136, 137, 174, 177
Harlow, H. F., 106, 110, 113, 118, 127, 143, 148, 152, 162
Harlow, M. K., 143, 148
Hartz, K. E., 139, 148
Hebb, D. O., 30, 31, 129, 135, 138, 157, 177
Heffner, H., 170, 174, 177
Henerey, M., 152
Herrnstein, R. J., 95, 97
Hess, E. H., 77, 92, 97, 134, 138
Hicks, L. H., 88, 97
Hill, R. M., 91, 97
Hinde, R. A., 4, 8, 66, 99
Hodos, W., 159, 162, 165, 166, 167, 170, 177, 188, 192
Horwich, R., 192
Howard, I. P., 77, 97
Hubel, D., 91, 97
Huidobro, F., 140, 148
Hunton, V. D., 88, 97

Ingle, D., 96, 97

Jenkins, W. O., 88, 98
Jennings, H. S., 103, 113, 183, 186

Jerison, H. J., 50, 52
Jones, L. V., 88, 97

Kellogg, W. N., 151, 152
Kennedy, J. L., 89, 98
Kettlewell, H. B. D., 29, 31
Keverne, E. B., 152
King, J. A., 166, 175, 176, 177
Krebs, D. L., 136, 138
Krechevsky, I., 123, 126
Köhler, W., 111

Lehrman, D. S., 66, 99, 157, 158, 177
Lemmon, W. B., 73, 98
Lester, D., 80, 98, 123, 125, 126, 171, 174, 175, 176, 177
Lester, G., 59, 66
Lilly, J., 143
Lindzey, G., 31, 138, 178, 192
Lockard, R. B., 170, 177
Lorenz, K., 133, 138, 158, 173, 177, 190, 192
Loveland, D. H., 95, 97
Lynn, R., 124, 127

Mabry, J., 186
MacLeod, M. C., 152
Maggiolo, C., 140, 148
Maier, B. M., 130, 137, 138
Maier, N. R. F., 38, 45, 64, 66, 172, 177
Maier, R. A., 130, 137, 138
Marler, P., 4, 8, 54, 61, 66, 174, 177
Marquis, D. G., 51, 52
Maslow, A. H., 118, 127
Mason, W. A., 118, 127
Masserman, J. H., 140, 143, 148
Masterton, B., 170, 174, 177
Matthiae, P. E., 192
Mayr, E., 9, 18, 20, 31
Mazokhin-Porshnyakov, G. A., 59, 66, 75, 81, 82, 92, 98
Mehlman, B., 181, 186
Menninger, K., 143, 148
Menzel, E. W., 76, 98, 159
Meyer-Holzapfel, M., 140, 148
Michael, R. P., 149, 152
Montagu, A., 16, 18, 142, 148
Morgan, C. T., 59, 66, 89, 98
Munn, N. L., 93, 98

Neiberg, A., 126, 127

Subject Index

203

Subject Index